Household Hints

Hilary Davies was born in Birmingham in 1949 and educated at King Edward VI High School and Newnham College, Cambridge. She has worked for British and American publishers since 1972, and for two years was a translator from French and German. She is now a publisher's editor.

Her household hints come from all sorts of sources, over many years: from a thrifty and practical family; from schooldays ('the first thing we were taught in Chemistry was how to pour our husbands' beer'); from holiday jobs as a chambermaid in the Austrian lakes, au pair in Vienna, kitchen maid in Denmark, and waitress in Wimbledon; from the experience of setting up house in first an old Dorset cottage and then a London flat; and from ingenious colleagues at work.

Her bad memory ('I have to write things down immediately or I just forget them'), combined with the need she has often felt for a handy 'emergency' guide to household facts and figures, have resulted in this book.

Hilary Davies

Household Hints

Fontana Paperbacks

First published by Fontana Paperbacks in 1981
Copyright © Hilary Davies 1981

Set in Lasercomp Times

Made and printed in Great Britain by
William Collins Sons & Co. Ltd, Glasgow

The hints in this book have been carefully
tested and presented, but as they are
intended only as possible solutions, the
author and publisher cannot be held
responsible for failure or resulting
damage.

For my mother

Contents

Introduction

If your problem is frozen pipes, or hard jam, or drooping houseplants, you need some household hints. If you're accident prone, if you tend to spill wine on new carpets and empty salt cellars into soup, you won't be safe without it. If you're mean (or hard up) and want to save money by making everything yourself, from yoghurt to hair conditioner, you can't afford to be without it. If you'd like to try some simple, old-fashioned cleaning aids like salt and vinegar instead of new-fangled things out of sprays; if you have treasures that need special care, whether old wood, ormolu or pearls; if you have blunt scissors or a dirty Oriental rug, moths in your carpet or dust in your violin; if your garden could be greener and your laundry whiter; if you've always wondered how to change a washer and a fuse, then *Household Hints* is exactly what you need.

The Storecupboard

Keep the following items in your cupboard and you will be well equipped to keep house – to clean, launder, remove stains from and maintain just about everything you can think of. Many of these items can be used instead of branded products and they are much less expensive. Remember to keep everything in your storecupboard labelled and dated, and above all follow the instructions on the packet.

From the chemist:

acetone
almond oil
aspirin
borax
castor oil
chamomile flowers
citric acid
coconut oil
cod liver oil
cream of tartar

denture cleaner
eucalyptus oil
formaldehyde
French chalk
fuller's earth
glycerine
gum arabic
hydrogen peroxide
kaolin

lanolin
lemon oil
oil of cloves
oil of lavender
oil of rosemary
petroleum jelly
rosewater
surgical spirit
witch hazel

From the ironmonger:

beeswax
candles
caustic soda
chalk
mild detergent
dry-cleaning
    solvent
household
    ammonia
household bleach
jeweller's rouge
lighter fuel

linseed oil
methylated spirit
paraffin
paraffin wax
pipe cleaners
plastic wood
powdered all-
    purpose filler
pure soft soap
sandpaper
shellac
soap flakes

starch
stove blacking
turpentine
vermiculite
washing soda
washing-up liquid
wax furniture
    polish
wax shoe polish
white spirit
wire wool

From the grocer:

baking powder
bicarbonate of
    soda
cider vinegar
cinnamon
    (powdered)

cloves
cornflour
lemon juice
mustard
    (powdered)

oatmeal
olive oil
white vinegar
wine vinegar

Caretaking

Taking care of things means more than just keeping them clean: it means knowing what's good for them. Anything that is particularly old, or fragile, or valuable – even if it's only sentimental value – needs special treatment. This chapter is a guide to that treatment. Did you know, for instance, that ivory likes to be in sunlight, and champagne corks shouldn't be allowed to pop? Did you know that cabbage leaves are good for pewter, and water bad for bronze? These hints will tell you the best and simplest ways of looking after your treasures: how to clean your silver with a lemon or how to freshen your carpet with a wipe of vinegar.

If you are the kind of person who likes to live with old-fashioned things, then you'll probably think it worthwhile to spend time and care keeping them in good condition – you'll get satisfaction out of seeing them look their best. Copper kettles and old lace, pine dressers and cast-iron stoves, suddenly brought out of storage into a harsh modern environment, need special attention – the kind of attention they used to get in the old days. So the gems that follow will help you to look after all sorts of family heirlooms – or junk shop bargains – with total confidence.

Ornaments

When transporting delicate pieces of china, glass and so on, wrap them first in damp newspaper. It will form a firm protective covering around them as it dries.

Pottery ornaments and ashtrays are liable to scratch highly polished surfaces. To prevent this, glue small pieces of felt or baize to their bases. Or use bits of self-adhesive foam rubber draught excluder, which you can buy in rolls from hardware shops.

Bronze

Bronze should not be washed. Dust carefully, then wipe with a soft cloth moistened with linseed oil. Dry in a warm place and polish with a chamois leather.

Candlesticks

Freeze candlesticks until the wax on them is quite hard. It can then be cracked off easily.

Copper and brass

Tarnished copper can be cleaned by rubbing with half a lemon dipped in salt, or with vinegar. Wash afterwards in soapy water, then polish.

Or, make a paste of equal amounts of flour and salt mixed with vinegar. Rub this on to tarnished brass or copper and leave to dry. Then rinse and polish with a soft cloth.

Small brass objects such as knobs from bedsteads, picture hooks and drawer handles can be cleaned by soaking overnight in household ammonia, then boiling in water in which haricot beans have been cooked. Allow to dry, then polish with a clean, soft cloth. Alternatively, soak in vinegar, rinse in hot water and dry off in a warm oven.

Eggs and how to suck them

The reason why Grandmother needed to know how to suck eggs was that she kept them as ornaments. Make sure that the eggs are newly laid. Using a scissor blade, make a hole in the sharp end about ⅓ inch (1 cm) in diameter. Stick a knitting needle into the egg to break the yolk and stir it. Then make a tiny hole at the blunt end using a pin and blow through this to force the contents out.

Fill a cup with water, stick the sharp end of the egg into it and suck at the smaller hole to force some water into the egg. Cover both holes with finger and thumb and shake the egg vigorously to rinse it. Repeat once or twice. Then immerse the egg completely in a strong solution of washing-up liquid and water. Rinse again. Wash the outside of the egg if necessary, using an old sterilized toothbrush, soap and water. It is then ready to be put on display – or decorated.

Ivory

Sunlight is good for ivory. Leave your ivory ornaments in a sunny place to keep them white (and leave the piano open so that sunlight can get to the keys).

Japanned ornaments

Japan is a hard varnish which gives wood a black, glossy finish. Wipe the surface with warm soapy water, dry, sprinkle with flour, leave for half an hour, then dust and polish.

Onyx

Sponge with methylated spirit.

Ormolu

Clean out of doors, preferably on a stone surface, and wear rubber gloves. Use a weak solution of household ammonia in warm water (see instructions on label for proportions), and then a mild liquid soap. Apply with balls of cotton wool (on cocktail sticks for small items). Rinse with clear warm water.

Pewter

Rub with petrol, dry, then rub with hot beer. Leave to dry, then buff with a clean cloth.

Or, polish with raw cabbage leaves.

Silver

The best way to clean silver is with jeweller's rouge (which you can buy from hardware shops) rubbed in by hand.

Or, rub used lemon halves over ornate silver, then wipe with a warm damp cloth and polish with a soft dry one.

Precious furniture

Antique wood

Antique wood should be waxed once a month with beeswax polish, made as follows:

> 2 oz (50 g) beeswax (i.e., 2 blocks)
> 2 oz (50 g) paraffin wax (or 2 household candles)
> 1 pint (500 ml) real turpentine
> 4 oz (100 g) pure soap (e.g., 'Fairy')
> 1 pint (500 ml) warm water

Grate the waxes, add them to the turpentine and leave to soak for twenty-four hours. Meanwhile grate the soap (to encourage it to dissolve), add it to the warm water, and leave this to soak for twenty-four hours as well.

When both the waxes and the soap are thoroughly dissolved, combine the two liquids and warm gently in a double boiler. (Make sure that the turpentine, which is highly inflammable, does not come into contact with a naked flame.)

Stir vigorously until an emulsion (it will look just like mayonnaise) is formed. Cool and store in a screw-top jar. Shake the polish before use, and apply sparingly.

Polish vigorously with clean, lint-free cloths (an old torn-up cotton sheet is ideal) until most of the wax has been absorbed into the wood. Repeat three or four times to get a rich, deep sheen.

To revive antique wood

To give a new lease of life to a neglected piece of wooden furniture, mix together in a screw-top jar equal parts of methylated spirit, linseed oil and vinegar. Shake vigorously before applying. Leave for four hours, then polish with a soft dry cloth.

This polish can be stored indefinitely; shake each time before using.

Carpets

You will not damage new carpets by vacuuming them, but you do risk clogging up your cleaner. Use a broom or a damp cloth for the first three weeks.

To revitalize a dingy old carpet, mix one part vinegar with three parts boiling water. Allow to cool. Dip a cloth into this solution, wring out well and rub the carpet gently. The faint smell of vinegar soon fades, and the colours in the carpet will look fresh and new.

Leather upholstery

Once or twice a year, apply wax shoe polish to leather upholstery to keep it supple. Polish off with a warm cloth.

Or, combine in a screw-top jar one part of wine vinegar with two parts of raw linseed oil. Shake vigorously and apply to the leather. Polish off with a silk handkerchief or a soft rag.

Puppy deterrent

Rub the legs of precious furniture with a little oil of cloves. The smell and bitter taste will discourage puppies from chewing them.

Other precious things

Champagne

To avoid accidents (and losing half the contents) take care

when opening a bottle of champagne not to let the cork pop. Popping means that the delicious fizz is escaping. In order to trap it, hold the bottle at an angle of forty-five degrees rather than upright. Ease the cork out gently by holding it still and turning the bottle slowly.

Earthenware

Before using a new unglazed earthenware casserole, season it by rubbing the outside with a cut onion or garlic clove. This will strengthen it so that it can withstand higher temperatures.

Earthenware casseroles are always liable to crack if boiling liquid is poured into them while they are cold. Warm them up gently first with running water. It is safer, when using them on top of the stove, to stand them on an asbestos mat.

Glasses

Put a metal spoon into a glass before pouring hot liquid into it (for instance when making Irish coffee), otherwise the glass may crack.

When washing precious glasses, place a clean, folded tea towel in the sink before adding the water, and another on the draining board to stand the glasses on when washed.

Ivory handles

Do not wash ivory or bone cutlery handles in hot water, which turns them yellow, but in lukewarm, slightly soapy water. Wipe them dry at once.

If they do get discoloured, wet them with soapy water and lay them in the sun for several hours.

Jewellery boxes

To give a wooden jewellery box a pretty sheen and pleasant smell, rub it with freshly-picked juicy leaves of lemon balm. Before the wood is dry polish it with a soft cloth.

Kilts

When packing a kilt or pleated skirt, roll it up lengthwise and thread it through one leg of an old pair of tights. It will arrive at its destination uncreased.

Leather bindings

The best way to keep leather-bound books in good condition is to take them off the shelf and read them. The oils in your skin will be sufficient to keep the leather supple. But if you haven't time to read them all, treat the bindings once or twice a year with wax furniture polish. This is particularly important in a centrally heated house.

To remove mould from leather book bindings and prevent it forming again, rub with oil of lavender. Sprinkle some oil on the bookshelves at the same time.

Leather shoes

Leather shoes take care of your feet and allow them to breathe. Take care of your shoes by always using a wax shoe polish.

Keep patent leather shoes or handbags supple by rubbing occasionally with a little petroleum jelly or olive oil.

Pearls

Real pearls should be worn as often as possible – even if they are kept out of sight, under a sweater or shirt – because they benefit from the skin's moisture and are liable to dry up without it.

Stringed instruments

If your violin, cello or guitar gets dusty, put a handful of uncooked rice inside it, shake it gently, then empty. The instrument will now be free of dust, and its tone much improved.

Cleaning

Some basic principles to bear in mind about cleaning:

Little and often. Don't allow dirt to build up: dust or wipe surfaces as frequently as possible and they will be easy to keep clean.

Look after your tools. Keep brooms and brushes clean by washing them in warm soapy water and then rinsing. They should be stored hanging up and not resting on their bristles, as this squashes them out of shape. Empty vacuum cleaner bags frequently, and do *not* wash cloth ones (see page 27). Wash dusters, chamois leathers and sponges frequently.

Look after your hands. If you wear rubber gloves for cleaning, buy a size larger than you need and wear a pair of thin cotton ones inside to absorb perspiration. If you don't wear gloves, scrape your fingernails along a bar of soap before tackling dirty jobs. After washing your hands apply a moisturizing lotion (page 48).

Start at the top. Always clean a room from top to bottom: the dirt you dislodge from walls, windows and furniture will be picked up when you get to the floor. The exception to this rule is cleaning paintwork (page 26).

Use polish sparingly. Remember, a good shine is 1 per cent polish and 99 per cent elbow grease.

The living-room

Bamboo

Clean with a soft brush dipped in salt water, dry with a soft cloth, and then rub in a little linseed oil. Dry in the sun if possible.

Cane chairs

Sponge with warm salt water, then rinse with clear warm water. If the seat is saggy, clean it first, then turn the chair upside down, saturate the cane with hot water. and dry in the sun.

Carpets

Dry shampoo your carpets by sprinkling oatmeal, cornflour or salt generously over them when they are looking dingy. Leave for a couple of hours, then vacuum.

Cast-iron stoves and fireplaces

Stove blacking is now available in tubes from good ironmongers. Wearing rubber gloves, apply it very sparingly to the stove or fireplace with a soft brush, then polish off with a medium-stiff brush or soft rag.

Rust can be removed by professional sand-blasting, to give a steely-grey finish.

Coconut matting

Beat well, then scrub with warm water and salt. Use soap as well if very dirty. Rinse and hang up (outside if possible) to dry.

Electric fires

An electric fire gives out far more heat if the reflector at the back is bright and shining. Give it an occasional rub with a silver cloth, or with impregnated wadding, and polish with a soft cloth.

Fabric lampshades

Dip in warm soapy water, brush with a soft brush, rinse and stand in a warm place to dry.

Floor polisher

Improvise a floor polisher by wrapping a duster round an old soft broom.

Gilt picture frames

Dust, then clean with a solution of three tablespoons of vinegar in one pint (500 ml) of cold water. Dry and polish with a soft cloth.

Leather furniture

Bring half a pint (250 ml) of linseed oil to boil, cool, and when nearly cold add half a pint (250 ml) of vinegar. Mix well and bottle. Rub this well into leather and polish with a soft cloth.

Mahogany

To remove bloom from mahogany, apply (after dusting) a solution of one tablespoon each of turpentine and linseed oil in two pints (1 litre) of warm water. Polish vigorously.

Or, clean with hot beer or hot tea before polishing.

Marble

Rub with a solution of one tablespoon each of salt and vinegar, leave for a few minutes (not longer), then wipe. Then rub with a cut lemon and wipe dry.

Mirrors

A few drops of methylated spirit on a damp cloth will give a beautiful depth and sparkle to mirrors. Polish afterwards with a soft dry cloth.

Oak

Wash with warm beer. While this is drying, boil a pint of beer with two teaspoons of sugar and a small piece of beeswax. Apply this mixture with a soft brush, and when it is dry polish with a chamois leather.

Oriental rugs

Modern cleaners or shampoos are liable to damage delicate Oriental rugs. The best way to clean them is to lay them face down on fresh snow and walk on them. Leave for a couple of hours, then vacuum or beat them and the colours will come up like new. If you can't find any snow, lay them on slightly damp grass instead.

Paintwork

Combine equal parts of water, methylated spirit and paraffin in a screw-top jar. Shake before using to polish paintwork and windows.

When washing paintwork always start at the bottom. If you start at the top the dirty water will drip downwards and be difficult to clean off. (This is one of those endless controversies, like whether or not to vacuum new carpets – see page 18. But in practice drips are easier to remove from a clean wall than a dirty one.)

Rugs

Hang on a clothes line and beat with a tennis racquet. Always beat the wrong side first, and then, more gently, the right side.

Slate

Clean with washing soda or milk. When the slate is dry, rub in a little lemon oil.

Stone floors and hearths

Do not use soap to clean stone, it will leave scum behind. Instead scrub with washing soda, then mop with clear water.

Tapestry

Sprinkle with fuller's earth, or with French chalk, and work this in with the fingertips or a clean cloth. Leave overnight, then brush (out of doors) with a soft clean brush.

Teak

Rub down very occasionally with extra fine (00 texture) wire wool and beeswax. Buff with a soft cloth.

Vacuum cleaners

Never wash the cloth bag of your vacuum cleaner: washing will make it porous.

Varnished floors

Clean with cold tea. (The tannin counteracts grease, and enhances the colour of the wood).

Wallpaper

Dirt can be removed from wallpaper by rubbing gently with stale bread or a soft India rubber.

Windows

The most effective window-cleaning tool is a chamois leather. And if your chamois leather needs cleaning, dissolve a teaspoonful of washing soda in a bowl of warm water and soak the leather in this for an hour. Wash in warm soapy water, then rinse. A dash of glycerine in the rinsing water will help to keep the leather soft.

Windows are easier to clean when they are steamy or damp.

A razor blade can be used gently to remove paint spots from windows, but be very careful not to scratch the glass. Alternatively, rub with hot vinegar.

Washing windows with a little vinegar in water makes the glass sparkle and also, in hot weather, helps to keep flies away.

If you haven't got a chamois leather, windows and mirrors can be cleaned by simply rubbing them with newspaper.

Wood-burning stoves

The mica windows of a wood-burning stove can be cleaned with vinegar and water.

Wooden furniture

If wooden furniture has become sticky with too much polish, apply a solution of half vinegar, half water. Rub off immediately with a dry cloth.

Remove the dust from the crevices of carved wooden furniture with a vacuum cleaner, or a small paint brush. Wipe with a cloth moistened in warm soapy water. Allow to dry, then apply a mixture of half turpentine, half liquid paraffin. Polish vigorously with a soft cloth.

Treat scratched or dry wooden surfaces by adding a little raw linseed oil to the beeswax polish (see page 17) – approximately two teaspoons to half a pint (250 ml) of polish. Apply thinly and buff up to a high gloss when dry.

The kitchen

Aluminium saucepans

Boil rhubarb or apple peelings in a stained aluminium pan and it will come up brilliantly clean.

Barbecue pans

Rub washing-up liquid on to the outsides of pans to be used for cooking over an open fire and allow to dry. They will be much easier to clean after use.

Burnt saucepans

Fill burnt saucepans with a strong solution of salt and water, leave overnight and then bring slowly to the boil: the burnt food should come away easily. Salt is better for this than washing soda because soda is liable to make the saucepan burn again next time it is used.

Butcher's block

Scrub vigorously with sawdust and a wire brush, as the butcher does. Then dust off with a soft brush.

Cake tins

Wash cake tins and other metal equipment while the oven is still warm, so that it can be used for drying them. This will stop them rusting.

To get rid of rust, rub cake tins with a cut raw potato dipped in scouring powder.

Cast-iron frying pans

Clean the outside with oven cleaning spray. Leave for two hours, then rub with vinegar and water.

Wash the inside in soapy warm water, dry, and rub in a little oil to prevent rust. If the pan does get rusty, use scouring powder or an impregnated pad to remove rust, then season again with oil.

Ceramic tiles

Clean with household ammonia in warm water.

Chopping board

Rub with a cut lemon to get rid of smells.

Chrome

Mix one part methylated spirit with two parts liquid paraffin. Apply with a damp cloth, polish with a dry one.

Decanters and vases

Soak overnight in denture cleaner.

Or, fill with household bleach in cold water and allow to stand until clean.

Or, fill with water and torn-up bits of newspaper. Leave overnight, rinse.

Or, fill with a solution of vinegar and water, and some small pebbles. Leave overnight, then rinse.

Gas cookers

Use pipe cleaners to clean the burner holes.

Glasses

To get glasses sparkling, wash them first in hot soapy water, rinse in cold clear water, and leave to dry.

Kettles

To descale a kettle fill it with water and a tablespoon of borax or citric acid (or vinegar or lemon juice). Bring to the boil and rinse.

Milk pans

Before boiling milk, rinse the saucepan in cold water to prevent the milk sticking.

After emptying the pan, wipe round the inside with a damp cloth or damp kitchen towel, and it will be much easier to clean later.

Mincers

After mincing meat, etc., clean the mincer by mincing stale bread in it.

Ovens

An easy – if extravagant – way to clean an oven is to turn the heat up very high for half an hour and burn off the dirt. Leave a window open to let out the smell. Then wipe with a hot damp cloth.

When the oven has just been used and is still hot, place a small bowl of household ammonia on the top shelf and a large bowl of boiling water on the bottom. Close the door and leave overnight. The next morning open the oven, remove bowls and leave to air for a few minutes before cleaning with soap and water.

After cleaning an oven thoroughly, rub a bicarbonate of

soda paste around it and the oven will be easier to clean next time. Make the paste by dissolving two tablespoons of bicarbonate of soda in two tablespoons of boiling water. Cool before use.

Oven shelves

Cover the shelves with silver foil to save cleaning so often. If they do get stained or burnt, put them in the bath and leave them to soak overnight in hot water and biological washing powder.

Quarry tiles

Apply linseed oil to new tiles to 'season' them. Keep them clean afterwards by wiping or scrubbing with warm soapy water.

Refrigerators

To get rid of mildew, wipe with vinegar.

Scrambled egg pan

Fill the pan with water after cooking scrambled eggs and add a dessertspoonful of dishwasher powder. Leave to soak for a quarter of an hour and the pan will be easy to clean.

Silver cutlery

Boil two pints (one litre) of water in a large saucepan with a tablespoonful of bicarbonate of soda. Drop cutlery (or other small silver items, such as napkin rings) in a few at a time, simmer for three minutes, then rinse and dry.

Teapots

To remove tannin stains, fill the teapot with a solution of

boiling water and a tablespoonful of washing soda or a little borax, or denture cleaning powder. Leave overnight, then wash.

Tea-stained china

Stubborn tea stains can be removed by rubbing with salt.

Thermos flask

Put a tablespoon of bicarbonate of soda in a stained Thermos flask, fill with hot water and leave overnight.

Waxed pine kitchen tables

Remove ingrained dirt by scrubbing with a stiff brush and scouring powder. Polish with a clean cloth. If necessary, re-wax (page 17).

Zinc

Wash in warm soapy water, then dry and rub with a cloth soaked in either turpentine or paraffin.

The bathroom

Baths

Pour boiling vinegar around the bath to remove hard water or dripping tap stains.

Lavatories

Make a paste of borax and lemon juice to remove stains or rings in the lavatory pan.

Shower curtains

Rub mildewed shower curtains with bicarbonate of soda or lemon juice. To prevent mildew forming again, soak in salted water before re-hanging.

Sponges

Real sponges should be washed in a solution of vinegar and warm water, then rinsed in cold water and hung outside to dry.

The dressing-room

Clothes brush substitute

Use sticky tape to remove dog hairs, fluff, etc. from dark clothes when you can't find a brush.

Combs

Add a few spoonfuls each of bicarbonate of soda and bleach to a bowl of warm water. Put combs into this for a few minutes, then swish around, rinse and leave to dry.

Costume jewellery

Soak overnight in denture cleaner. Next morning brush gently with a soft toothbrush. Do not use this treatment for pearls or precious stones.

Diamonds

Clean with gin.

Felt hats

Make a paste with white spirit and French chalk. Rub well into the hat, leave to dry, then brush off.

Fur coats

Sprinkle with fuller's earth or talcum powder, roll up and leave overnight in a warm place. Then shake and brush gently in the direction of the fur.

Or, cover with unwaxed brown paper and iron very lightly with a warm iron in the direction of the fur.

Hairbrush

Add a little baking soda or household ammonia to a small basinful of cold water. Dip the bristles of the brush in this without letting the back get wet. After a few minutes rinse in clear water, shake vigorously and lay the brush on its side to dry, preferably in fresh air. Never wash a hairbrush in hot water and never lay it on its back to dry.

Kid gloves

Surface dirt may be removed with a soft India rubber.

Shoes

You need three brushes for use with tinned polish: a stiff one, for brushing off mud; a soft one, for applying the polish; and a medium one, for polishing.

To get salt out of shoes rub with half vinegar, half water solution, then dry and brush.

Straw hats

Wipe with a cloth squeezed out of soapy water, then bleach

with a mixture of one teaspoon of salt and one tablespoon of lemon juice. Rinse in cold water and dry in the sun.

Suede

Sprinkle with oatmeal or fuller's earth, leave for an hour or two and brush with a soft brush.

Miscellaneous

Candles

Wipe with a cloth dipped in methylated spirit.

Dogs

If your dog hates baths, rub bicarbonate of soda into his coat to act as a dry shampoo-cum-flea-deterrent. Brush out thoroughly.

Playing cards

Remove dirt and grease by rubbing with bread.

Sewing machines or typewriters

Remove dust from inside with the crevice tool of a vacuum cleaner, then clean with methylated or surgical spirit.

Stuffed toys

Rub cornflour into the fur, leave for half an hour, then brush.

Telephones

Clean with methylated or surgical spirit.

Thrift

If you want to save money:

Don't throw anything away without first considering if it can be transformed or re-used (see 'Recycling'). See this section for suggestions about old newspapers, tea leaves, coffee grounds, hot water bottles, even old pyjama legs.

If it seems to have gone off – if jam goes sugary, or shoe polish hard, or breakfast cereal soft – you will find here a simple way to 'refresh' it.

Get the most out of it. Drain bottles to the last dregs. Use every bone in the chicken, all the vitamins in the vegetables. Find out how to make soap and candles and rubber gloves last longer, make tea stronger, lemons and cream go further.

Make it yourself instead of buying commercial products. Make your own beauty treatments (see pages 47–50), muesli, stock, curry powder and yoghurt. You'll know exactly what's in them – they're purer and far less expensive than branded goods.

Save fuel. Whatever heating temperature you are used to, turn it down. Heat only the rooms that you use, fill the kettle with only as much water as you need. Lose pounds from your heating bills by insulating the loft but look after the pennies too by taking hints about fuel-saving in the kitchen.

Recycling

Brown paper

Save money and help to save trees by opening out the 'tree saver' bags given away in supermarkets and using the paper to wrap parcels.

Firelighters

Empty milk cartons, well rinsed and stored flat to save space, make excellent firelighters, and dried potato peelings can be used to kindle a fire.

Or, light a fire using 'logs' made from rolls of newspaper tied into knots. They will be even more effective if wetted before rolling and then dried.

Or, save dead wooden matches. When you have a boxful it can be used for kindling a fire.

Hot water bottles

To make a rubber hot water bottle last longer, add a few drops of glycerine the first time you fill it.

Don't throw away an old leaking hot water bottle: use it as a kneeling pad for indoor floor scrubbing or outdoor weeding. Cut the top off, stuff with old cut-up tights, and seal the end with sticky tape.

Stoneware hot water bottles can be used as candle holders, or converted into table lamps with a cork-based fitment.

Ironing board cover

A leg cut from a discarded pair of pyjama bottoms can be used as an ironing board cover.

Orange boxes

In the evening when street markets are packing up, collect discarded orange boxes and use them as stacking coffee tables, or, hung sideways on the wall, as display shelves.

Pin cushions

Pin cushions can be stuffed with used dried coffee grounds; the pins stored in them will never go rusty.

Sheets and towels

Cut up worn-out sheets to make pillowcases or dusters; towels to make face cloths.

Wood ash

Save the clean white ash left by a wood fire. It can be used as a scouring powder for stained china, or as a garden fertilizer (see page 137).

Thrifty cleaning

Cleaning powder

Sprinkle cleaning powder or liquid on to a cloth, not on to the surface you are cleaning, and you will use far less of it.

Pan scourer

Screwed up tin foil can be used for scouring pans.

Rubber gloves

The hand you use more tends to wear out faster than the other – unless you turn the gloves inside out sometimes and wear them on opposite hands.

Scouring pads

Cut steel wool pads in half and they will last longer.

Scuffed shoes

Use a felt-tip pen to disguise scuff marks on children's shoes.

Shoe polish

If shoe polish goes hard and cracks, put the tin into the oven or stand it over a gentle heat for a few minutes and it will soften.

Soap

When you buy a new bar of soap, take it out of the packet to dry out for a few days before using it. It will last much longer. Keep it in a clothes drawer until you need it: it will make your clothes smell nice.

It simply isn't necessary to buy shaving soap. Ordinary soap works just as well.

Washing-up liquid

Don't pretend to yourself that you're saving money by buying cheap washing-up liquid: you know you'll have to use five times as much to get the same lather.

Instead, when you buy a new container of washing-up liquid, decant half of it into another container and fill up with water. At half-strength it will be perfectly effective and last twice as long.

Thrift in the kitchen

Bacon rinds

Fry bacon rinds and use them to add flavour to soups.

Dried beans

To save time and fuel when preparing dried beans, peas, etc. for cooking, first wash them thoroughly, then put in a saucepan with plenty of cold water, cover, bring to the boil and simmer for five minutes. Leave to soak overnight or as long as possible: the longer they soak the less cooking they will need.

Do *not* add bicarbonate of soda to the water – this breaks down the vitamins in the beans.

Bottle-emptying

To get the last drops out of a bottle of sauce, hand cream, etc., stand the bottle in hot water for a minute. The contents will then pour out easily.

Bread

Dip a stale loaf in cold water, then heat it in the oven until it is dry. Wrap in a damp cloth and cool.

Or, wrap in foil and bake in the oven at gas mark 8, 450°F, 230°C, for ten minutes.

Breakfast cereal

Soft, stale cereals (and ice cream wafers) can be made crisp again by being heated in a warm oven or under the grill for a few minutes.

Home-made cayenne pepper

Remove the stalks from an ounce (25 g) of red chilli peppers and dry them in a slow oven until crisp. Pound them in a mortar with a quarter of their weight of salt. Store in a screw-top jar.

Chicken stock

Never throw a chicken carcass away. Put it in a large saucepan, cover with cold water, and simmer for at least an hour with an onion, a carrot, a stick of celery, a bay leaf, parsley and thyme (or as many of these as you happen to have) to make a delicious chicken stock.

Chocolate

If you butter a pan or bowl thoroughly before melting chocolate in it, less chocolate will stick and be wasted.

Christmas pudding

Press left-over pudding into a small basin while still hot to make a 'new' pudding.

Cream

When whipping cream for desserts, use half single and half double cream with a little caster sugar added. Alternatively, add two egg whites beaten stiffly with caster sugar to a small carton of double cream.

Home-made curry powder

> ½ teaspoon cayenne pepper
> ½ teaspoon cloves
> 2 teaspoons allspice
> 2 teaspoons ginger
> 3 teaspoons cinnamon
> 3 teaspoons cumin seeds
> 3 teaspoons fennel seed
> 4 teaspoons turmeric
> 5 teaspoons black pepper
> 11 teaspoons coriander seeds

All ingredients should be freshly ground.

Dandelion salad

Take a bunch of dandelion leaves and drop them in a large pan of boiling water for one minute. (This gets rid of the bitter flavour.) Drain and cool. Add chopped fresh herbs and toss in an oil-and-vinegar dressing.

Distilled water

Instead of buying distilled water to use in steam irons and car batteries, use the melted water from a defrosted refrigerator.

Egg boxes

Plastic egg boxes can be used for making ice in. Also for freezing mint sauce or first-size baby meals in.

Greaseproof paper

Keep butter wrappers for greasing and lining cake tins, and covering joints of meat while roasting.

Herbal tea

Pour a pint (500 ml) of boiling water on to an ounce (30 g) of fresh herbs or half that weight of dried herbs. Cover and leave for six minutes, then strain.

Home-made icing sugar

To save buying icing sugar, grind granulated sugar in the grinder attachment of a blender until it is of the right powdery consistency. If you grind it half as much you will have caster sugar.

Jam

If an opened jar of jam or honey goes hard and sugary, stand it in a saucepan of water and heat it gently.

Lamb dumplings

Half-cook a lamb stew the day before it is required, and the fat which hardens on top of it can be used to make delicious dumplings. To make about 16 dumplings, combine 2 oz (50 g) fat with 4 oz (100 g) self-raising flour, half a small onion finely chopped, salt, pepper and chopped fresh or dried herbs including mint and rosemary. Bind with a little cold water to make an elastic dough, divide into teaspoonfuls, roll in flour into balls and simmer in stew or soup for fifteen to twenty minutes.

Lemon juice

If you need only a few drops of juice from a whole lemon,

pierce the fruit with a knitting needle instead of cutting it in half.

A lemon heated for a few minutes in the oven before squeezing will yield twice as much juice.

Home-made muesli
To serve 4:

> 1 mugful rolled oats
> 2 tablespoons chopped hazelnuts
> 2 tablespoons raisins
> 1 tablespoon pumpkin or sesame seeds
> 1 chopped apple
> 1 teaspoon lemon juice
> soft brown sugar to taste

Add milk and stir; leave for five minutes before eating.

Pease pudding

Soak half a pound (250 g) of split green peas overnight, then tie them in a piece of muslin and immerse them in a panful of boiling salted water. Add a ham bone and simmer, covered, for two hours or until the peas are tender. Sieve them and add an ounce (25 g) of butter, a beaten egg, and seasoning. Tie in a floured cloth and simmer for thirty minutes more. Serve with ham or bacon.

Tea

Warm tea leaves in the oven for a few minutes before use to bring out a fuller flavour and make the tea go further.

Free vegetables

Wearing leather or rubber gloves, pick a large bunch of young nettle tops. Wash several times, remove stalks, and cook for ten minutes in a little boiling water. Strain and serve with butter.

Vegetable water

Keep the water in which vegetables have been boiled and use it in soups and stocks. It is full of vitamins.

Waxed paper

Save the waxed paper from cornflake packets. It can be used to line cake tins and wrap food in.

Left-over wine

Pour left-over wine into a screw-top or corked jar and keep for cooking.

Wine substitute

Dry cider can successfully be substituted for wine in cooking.

To make yoghurt

Warm a pint (500 ml) of sterilized milk to just below boiling point, but do not boil. Cool to blood heat – 98·4°F, 37°C. This is important: if the milk is hotter it will kill the yoghurt bacteria. Add to the milk a tablespoon of live yoghurt or shop-bought natural yoghurt. If this is at all watery, add a heaped tablespoon of dried milk as well. Place the mixture in an airing cupboard or warm place overnight. Repeat daily for a constant supply.

Thrifty beauty

Body lotion

Mix glycerine and rosewater in equal proportions, and smoothe gently into the skin before going to bed.

Coconut oil conditioner

Use coconut oil to condition dull splitting hair. Massage it thoroughly into the scalp, then wrap in a hot towel. Re-heat the towel (by wringing it out of very hot water) as soon as it begins to cool, and continue re-heating and wrapping for half an hour. Then rinse.

Dry shampoo

Sprinkle cornflour or baby powder on to dirty or greasy hair, then brush out.

Face pack for a dry complexion

Mix one egg yolk with a few drops each of olive oil and lemon juice. Spread this on your face after washing thoroughly. Leave for ten minutes while you lie down and relax, then rinse off with cold water.

Face pack for a greasy complexion

Beat an egg white until stiff, then fold in two tablespoons of cornflour. Spread this over your face and leave until it feels dry and tight. Remove gently with a dry cloth, and rinse with cold water.

Freckle treatments

Soak fresh elderberries in distilled water overnight. Strain and use the liquid for washing your face. Repeat daily.

Or, mix a tablespoonful of milk with a teaspoonful of freshly grated horseradish. Leave to stand for an hour before applying to the face. Repeat daily.

Hair rinse

To get rid of the last vestiges of shampoo after washing and make your hair beautifully shiny, add to the final rinsing water a tablespoon of lemon juice (for blondes) or a tablespoon of cider vinegar (for brunettes).

Hair rinse for blondes

Make chamomile tea by pouring half a pint (250 ml) of boiling water over two teaspoonfuls of dried chamomile flowers or a handful of fresh ones. Leave to brew for ten minutes, then use this to rinse fair hair after shampooing.

Hand lotion

Mix two parts of glycerine with one part of lemon juice. Massage gently into the hands after washing.

Hand softener

Mix a teaspoon of olive oil with a teaspoon of granulated or caster sugar and rub well into the hands for a few minutes until the sugar has dissolved.

Herbal hair conditioner

You will need:

1 tablespoon almond oil
1 tablespoon glycerine
1 tablespoon lanolin
a few drops of oil of rosemary
1 egg

Combine the first four ingredients in a saucepan and heat gently. Remove from heat and beat in the egg.

Massage into the scalp after shampooing, leave for ten minutes, then rinse.

Medicines

It is far cheaper to buy the BP (British Pharmacopoeia) product – such as aspirin or petroleum jelly – than the commercial equivalent. Consult your pharmacist.

Nail varnish

When nail varnish gets too thick and sticky to use, stand it for a few minutes in a saucepan of boiling water.

Nail varnish remover

Add a few drops of castor oil to a bottle of pure acetone (both available from a chemist).

Setting lotion

Add a teaspoonful of sugar to half a pint (250 ml) of hot water. Cool until comfortable to use.

Skin freshener

Combine equal parts of rosewater and witch hazel. Dab on to the complexion with cotton wool after washing.

Spot lotion

Dab frequently with lemon juice.

Toothpowder

Bicarbonate of soda makes an excellent and inexpensive toothpowder.

Saving fuel

Baked and roast potatoes

Boil potatoes for five minutes before baking or roasting.

A cup of tea

Instead of making a whole pot of tea when you need only one cup, put a teaspoonful of tea into a strainer on a cup, pour boiling water through it and leave the strainer in place for two minutes to let the tea brew.

Gas burners

There is no point in having a gas ring turned up so high that the flames lick the sides of a saucepan – this heat is only wasted.

Hot water

Do not overfill a kettle; heat only as much water as you need.

Insulating floors

Fill gaps between your floorboards with strips of draught excluder before laying carpets.

Mashed potatoes

Cut potatoes into small pieces before boiling them to mash.

Saucepans

Always cook in the smallest possible pan on the smallest suitable ring at the lowest convenient temperature.

Thrifty toast

If your grill will take only two pieces of bread at a time and you want to make toast for three, save time and fuel by grilling as follows (1, 2 and 3 are the pieces of toast; A and B are the two sides): 1A, 2A; 3A, 1B; 2B, 3B. (This may sound complicated but it isn't. What you are doing is using the grill three times instead of four.)

Underfelt

A thick layer of newspaper can be used for insulation under a carpet instead of underfelt.

Water heater

Do not overheat your water. Set the thermostat at 55° C, 113° F.

Miscellaneous thrift

Beer

Before opening a bottle of beer, bang sharply three times on the lid. This will stop the contents bursting out when the lid is loosened.

When pouring beer, tip the glass towards the bottle so that

the beer flows gently down the side of the glass instead of hitting the bottom.

Candles

Freeze candles before use and they will last much longer.

Home-made glue

Boil a pint (500 ml) of water in a saucepan and dissolve in it an ounce (25 g) of borax. Add two ounces of shellac, and continue simmering, covered, until the shellac has dissolved.

Missing plugs

A missing bath or sink plug can be temporarily replaced by a coin wrapped in a handkerchief folded to the required thickness.

Modelling dough

Combine three cups of flour, one cup of salt, one cup of water and a little food colouring to make children's modelling dough. Knead the mixture well. If stored in a polythene bag it will last for several days.

Stair carpets

When laying a stair carpet allow an extra half yard or half metre to be folded under at the top or bottom, so that the carpet can be moved when it begins to wear.

Do-It-Yourself

This chapter won't tell you much about plumbing and wiring and fancy joints, but it does set out some of the most basic and useful rules about things like saws and drills and sandpaper. It tells you how to change a washer and mend a fuse, make instant repairs and paint and paper quickly and neatly. When you've mastered these you can have fun knocking together a window box (page 136) or framing pictures (page 57) or just putting up shelves (page 60).

Some do-it-yourself rules:

Get to know your materials, whether wood, plaster, paper or paint. Learn how wood likes to be sanded, sawn, planed and primed, how it responds to moisture and heat. Learn how to make paint more manageable, how to store it, how to stop it getting everywhere you don't want it.

Learn basic techniques like how to drill a good hole, and how to fill one; how to hold a saw, and how to cut card. Learn how to apply paint most efficiently, with either a brush or a roller.

Look after your tools so that they don't get rusty: wipe cutting edges with oil before you put them away; store nails and screws in airtight containers. Keep each tool in its place, and store different items separately, so that you can pick up what you need at a glance (see page 92).

Changing a plug

An easy way to remember which colour wire to attach to which plug terminal is: hold the plug upright with the pins away from you. The wire which goes to the left pin is blue, and 'l' for 'left' is the second letter of 'blue'. The wire which goes to the right pin is brown, and 'r' for 'right' is the second letter of 'brown'.

Changing a washer

Buy from a plumber's merchant or ironmonger a new washer of the appropriate size. Turn the water off at the mains and turn on the faulty tap to allow all the water to drain out of the pipe. Then wrap the tap in a cloth to protect it while you remove the handle and the body casing using a spanner.

Undo the nut, remove the old washer, and replace it with the new one. Put the tap back together again.

If you have a modern 'Supatap' you will not need to turn the water off at the mains first.

China

When mending china lightly grease the outside of the object around the cracked edges. If glue oozes out from the join the grease will prevent it from setting and it can easily be wiped away.

When a piece of china has broken into more than two pieces, always stick them all together at the same time.

Hold the pieces together with masking tape while they set.

To repair chipped china, warm a little epoxy resin adhesive in a slow oven to make it runnier and mix it thoroughly with a little kaolin. Dip a small palette knife into methylated spirit and use this to apply the mixture to the chip, shaping it as required. When dry, smooth down with sandpaper. Paint, then apply polyurethane varnish.

Cutting card

When cutting card with a Stanley knife and a steel straight-edge, the golden rule for safety and efficiency is to lean heavily on the straight-edge and lightly on the knife.

Cutting leather

If you need to cut leather, soak it first in water to soften it.

To darken wood

To bring out the lovely natural colour and grain of newly-sanded floorboards, etc., rub in neat linseed oil. When dry, shine well with beeswax polish (see page 17).

Drilling

When drilling a solid wall, instead of pressing violently on the drill all the time, which will probably wear you down before the wall, set up a steady rhythm, applying pressure for several seconds and then relaxing.

If you put an extension lead on your electric drill (or any other electric tool), remember that the so-called 'masculine', pronged half of the connecting plug must be attached to the drill and the 'feminine' half attached to the extension.

When drilling a slippery surface such as ceramic tiles or metal, cover the area first with insulation tape.

When plugging a brick wall, drill the hole at the bottom of the brick where it is solid across the whole width.

To fill a gap

Make a putty-like mixture with powdered all-purpose filler and white undercoat paint. Pack this into a gap between a bath or washbasin and wall and smooth down with a knife. After a few days it will have set hard and can be sanded down and painted.

To finish white-wood furniture

Save money by buying unfinished white-wood furniture and finishing it yourself. Rub down with progressively finer sandpaper. Brush off every trace of dust. Apply one coat of linseed oil with a lint-free cloth, and when dry polish with wax furniture polish.

Floor coverings

Brush the cut edges of carpet or rush matting with latex adhesive to prevent fraying.

A small hole in lino can be filled with a few drops of wax from a candle of the same colour. Press the wax firmly into the hole, allow to harden, then polish.

Framing pictures

Buy old frames from junk shops or jumble sales. Clean gilt ones (see page 62); strip (see page 25) and polish or paint wooden ones.

The plain card which surrounds a framed picture is called a mount. To make a mount buy mounting card from an artist's supply shop and cut it to fit easily inside the frame (see page 55, 'cutting card'), then cut a rectangular (or whatever shape the picture is) opening in the middle by placing the picture on top of the mount and making pin pricks at the four corners to go through on to the card as a guide for the size and position of the opening. (The opening should usually be a quarter of an inch – just less than a centimetre – smaller all round than the picture, so as to cover the edges. To be visually pleasing the mount should be slightly wider at the bottom than the top.)

Draw the shape of the opening on the mounting card. Using a Stanley knife and a steel straight-edge, cut along this line at an angle of forty-five degrees, sloping inwards towards the centre of the opening.

If you wish, rule fine pen lines around the mount for emphasis.

To assemble, place the frame face down on a soft cloth on a flat surface. Drop in the glass (cleaned with methylated spirit), then the picture and mount. Cover with a piece of hardboard cut to the same size as the mount and tack this to the frame using $\frac{1}{2}$-inch (12 mm) steel pins 1 inch (2·5 cm) apart. Or use sticking plaster. Finally cover with a piece of brown paper and stick this to the frame with parcel tape.

Fix two screw-eyes to the back of the frame and thread cord or picture wire through them.

Fuses in plugs

Use a red 3-amp fuse in a plug on appliances up to 720W, such as lamps, food mixers, electric blankets; and brown 13-amp fuses for appliances over 720W and up to 3000W, such as kettles, irons, radiant fires, washing machines. Colour televisions, vacuum cleaners and freezers *may* need 13-amp fuses; but always check manufacturer's instructions.

Hanging pictures

Use old sewing machine needles or picture-hooks with fine pins rather than nails, as they are less likely to crack plaster. A piece of sticky tape also helps to stop plaster cracking.

Holes in wood

If you fill holes in wood with putty instead of powdered filler you will find that gloss paint applied over them remains glossy instead of being absorbed.

To mend a fuse

Keep a supply of fuse wires – 5 amp for lighting, 15 amp for heating and 30 amp for cookers – together with a torch and screwdriver near to the fusebox. Get to know your fusebox – find out which fuse is which.

When a fuse blows, switch off the electricity at the mains. If you know what made the fuse blow – if you just plugged in an appliance which may be faulty, or overloaded a socket – deal with this problem by unplugging the appliance(s).

Take out and inspect the fuses in the fusebox one at a time until you find the one that has blown (the wire has snapped). Using the screwdriver remove the old wire, cut a new piece of the appropriate wire and insert this. Replace the fuse. Turn on at the mains.

Nails

If nails are too short to hold, stick them through a piece of card first, then hold that while banging the nailhead. The card can be torn away afterwards.

Plastic

A small crack in plastic can be repaired by running a hot (not quite red-hot) screwdriver lightly along it.

To remove French polish

Rub with wire wool dipped in methylated spirit.

To remove lacquer from brass

To strip down an old piece of lacquered brass – such as a bedstead – rub with surgical spirit. Do not use paint stripper.

Sanding

Always sand with the grain of wood, otherwise you will scratch it.

Sandpaper should always be wrapped round a block of wood (and held together with sticky tape) so as to give an even surface.

Sawing

Keep a piece of candle in your tool box and before sawing wood rub the candle a couple of times along each side of the blade. This makes sawing much easier. The work of sawing is done on the downward stroke. This is when to apply pressure.

When sawing plywood, stick masking tape along the line to be cut to prevent the plywood splintering.

Screws

To stop screws rusting and ease removal later, dip the tips in petroleum jelly.

Brass and chrome screws are not very strong, so if you need to insert them in wood make a hole with a wood screw of the same size first.

To put up shelves in an alcove

If you need adjustable shelves on a straight wall to carry heavy weights it is probably most sensible to use metal brackets that fit into slots in vertical metal strips. In this case, follow the manufacturer's instructions for assembly. But if you have some empty alcoves and you don't want to be able to adjust the height of your shelves, you can support them on neat wooden batons instead of brackets.

First of all, take the measurements using a metal rule in both inches and centimetres (in case your timber merchant has not yet gone metric). Measure the length of each shelf individually, as alcoves vary in width from top to bottom *and* from back to front.

Then measure the length of the batons you will need. If the shelves are to take a lot of weight you should put a baton at the back of each shelf as well as at the sides. The side batons should be slightly shorter than the width of the shelves, so that they are not obtrusive.

If you buy pine shelving it will probably be $\frac{3}{4}$ inch (2·5 cm) thick, and the timber merchant should cut it to the lengths you want. If he won't, go to one who will. The batons should be about $\frac{1}{2}$ inch (1·5 cm) thick and $\frac{3}{4}$ inch (2·5 cm) wide. Wood this width comes in long strips that you can saw up yourself.

For a normal masonry wall you will need two 1$\frac{1}{2}$ inch (3·5 cm) screws for each side baton and three each for the back ones – more if the shelves are to be exceptionally long. You will also need the same number of rawlplugs; some quick-setting fibrous filler in case of emergencies; a saw; an electric drill with a wood-drilling bit slightly fatter than the neck of the screws; a counter-sink bit for hollowing out a nest for the screw heads; a masonry bit, again slightly fatter than the screws; sandpaper; a spirit level; a hammer; a screwdriver; and a pencil.

Cut the batons into the lengths you need and neaten the ends with sandpaper. Mark the positions for the screws and drill straight holes and then counter-sink holes for them. Draw carefully on the wall, using the spirit level, a line indicating where the top of each baton should go, then offer the batons up and, poking a sharp point through each screw hole, mark the wall where each screw should go.

Using the masonry bit, drill the holes in the wall deep enough for the rawlplugs to go right in: they must not protrude at all. Tap them in with a hammer: they must fit tightly. Then hold the baton in place and insert the screws, giving them a few turns by hand first to check that the holes are correctly positioned. Tighten with a screwdriver.

Sand the ends of the shelves if they are rough and, if you wish, finish them with linseed oil (see page 56). Then simply lodge them in place.

The handiest hint is to complete each process one at a time – do all of the sawing at once, all the wood drilling at once, and so on, rather than putting up one shelf at a time. Otherwise you will be constantly changing drill bits and reaching for different tools.

To splice a tape

A spot of nail varnish remover will hold two ends of cassette tape together.

To strip painted pine

Working outside and wearing protective clothing, add one tin (500 g) of caustic soda to two pints (1 litre) of cold water in a metal bucket, according to the directions on the tin.

Pour this on to one surface at a time of the object to be stripped, leave for a few seconds, then rub in with an old long-handled scrubbing brush. Repeat as often as necessary until all the paint is loosened.

Now pour clean water over the wood and scrub until all paint is removed. Wipe with a weak vinegar and water solution, then leave to dry slowly – out of doors if possible.

When completely dry, sand the wood with progressively finer sandpaper. Fill cracks with plastic wood and sand again, then apply two coats of shellac to protect the wood against dry heat. Rub this into the grain with fine wire wool.

Finish with beeswax polish (see page 17).

Wall plugs

Short lengths of hollow plastic washing line, or matches, can be used instead of wall plugs.

Wiring colours

The new wiring colours are blue for neutral; green or green and yellow for earth; brown for live.

The old colours were: black for neutral; green for earth; red for live.

Decorating

Paint and painting

Add a tablespoon of white spirit to a large tin of gloss paint to make it more manageable and stop drips forming.

Strain lumpy paint through muslin or nylon stockings.

To prevent a skin forming on gloss paint left in a tin, store the tin upside down. Thixotropic (non-drip gloss) paint should be shaken vigorously before being put into storage.

When painting a room cover taps and doorknobs with plastic bags held on with rubber bands so that you don't get paint on them.

Drip catching. When you are painting a ceiling with a brush, push the handle through a paper plate to catch drips of paint.

Obstacles. When you get to the ceiling rose above a light simply unscrew it and paint close to the cable, instead of trying to paint round it. Similarly, unscrew a light switch – but remember to switch the electricity off at the mains first.

Skirting boards. Stick masking tape or Sellotape on to the carpet next to the skirting board before painting it. Or slide a piece of cardboard, wood or metal along as you work.

Touching up. When you have finished painting, pour a little left-over paint into an empty nail varnish bottle to use for small touching up jobs. Make sure the bottle and its brush have been thoroughly cleaned first with acetone.

Windows. When painting window frames stick masking tape around panes of glass to avoid getting paint on them; or use a straight-sided piece of cardboard or metal, as for skirting boards.

Slide a Stanley knife down next to the frame to loosen a window that has been painted shut.

If old windows are so thick with paint that they will no longer close easily, apply paint stripper to the edges. Then prime and paint again. Remember to leave them open until dry.

Paint brushes

To prevent emulsion paint hardening on a brush during a short break or overnight, wrap the brush tightly in kitchen foil; *or*, wrap it in a cloth and place it in the freezer. To prevent gloss paint hardening, suspend the brush in a jar of water or, better still, paraffin.

Drill holes in paint brush handles so that they can be hung up when not in use – or suspended in cleaning solution – rather than left standing on their bristles.

If paint brushes have gone stiff in storage you can soften them by submerging the bristles for several minutes in a pan of boiling vinegar.

Plaster

Always add plaster to water, not water to plaster.

Wallpaper and wallpapering

Always buy – or reserve at the shop – one more roll of paper than you think you need. You will almost certainly use more than you think, and the dye used in different batches may vary.

When you have finished wallpapering a room, write in some inconspicuous place (such as behind a picture) how many rolls of paper you used so that you will know next time.

To remove old wallpaper, wet it thoroughly with warm water. When it begins to blister you can peel it off quite easily. It is best to work on only a small area – say a couple of widths of paper – at a time, otherwise the paper will dry again before you can remove it.

Always start wallpapering next to a window and work away from it. When you get to a convenient stopping place, such as a door, start again from the other side of the window, working round the room in the opposite direction. You will find that the joins are less noticeable if you do this, because of the way the light falls on them.

Corners. When wallpaper needs to be pleated to fit in awkward corners or over bulges, tear it rather than cut it. An uneven tear will be less noticeable. Hold the paper firmly against the wall and tear towards you: the edge you pull towards you should then be stuck on top of the other.

Matching. Keep a small swatch of curtain material, a cutting of wallpaper and a square cut from a paint colour chart pasted on to a card while shopping for accessories.

Paste. Tie a piece of string across your paste bucket for wiping excess paste off the brush, and also to act as a support for the brush when not in use.

When you have finished wallpapering, pour a little left-over paste into a screw-top jar to use for corners of paper that come loose and for minor repairs.

Patching. Hang a strip of left-over paper in the back of your wardrobe after papering a room. If you need to patch, this will have faded to the same shade as that on the walls.

Needlework

Some first principles:

A good light is essential for sewing and knitting. If you are right-handed sit with the source of light over your left shoulder, and vice versa, so that you are not sewing in your own shadow. If the light is still not adequate, arrange a white cloth on your lap or under the arm of your sewing machine to act as a reflector.

Know your materials so that you choose the fabric or yarn

most suitable for the article you want to make – easily washable fibres for children's clothes, cotton for summer clothes, wool for winter.

A stitch in time of course saves tempers fraying as well as holes. Carry out minor repairs before they become major – certainly before laundering, which tends to turn small holes into big ones. Sew on buttons before you lose them; replace them when you take the garment off rather than remembering them just as you are about to put it on.

Keep your work-box tidy. Store pins and needles in a rust-proof pin cushion (see page 39) or in an airtight container. Thread reels of cotton on to a loop of covered wire or keep them in something like a plastic cutlery tray so that you can see them all at once and they don't get in a tangle.

Buttonholes

Before cutting a buttonhole, apply a line of colourless nail varnish to prevent fraying.

Curtains

New curtains tend to grow longer after hanging for a few weeks, so the hems should at first only be tacked up.

When sewing in curtain linings, in order to prevent the stitches going through to the right side, insert a strip of cardboard between the curtain and the lining and slide it along as you sew. Remember to remove it afterwards.

Cutting nylon

Heat scissors before cutting nylon: this helps to seal the edges of the material.

Darning

If you haven't got a darning mushroom, use an electric light bulb instead.

Deckchair cover

Use a double length of canvas and fit on to the deckchair like a roller towel, without nailing. The seat will be stronger and can be moved round as it wears.

Flimsy material

When sewing very delicate fabric by machine, place tissue paper underneath seams. This can be gently torn off afterwards.

Hems

To get hems level, put the skirt or dress on and have it measured from the floor with a marked stick.

The same method can be used for levelling curtain hems by measuring from the floor or window sill.

To save marking a delicate fabric by pinning or tacking a hem in place, mark the fold-line with tailor's chalk and use hairpins or paper clips to hold the hem in place for sewing.

Letting down jeans

If you are left with a worn white line after lengthening jeans, camouflage it by applying a line of watered-down blue ink with a small brush.

Needles and threads

Prevent thread slipping out of a needle by sewing once through the thread itself.

It is quicker (when sewing easily manageable fabrics) to use a short needle.

To thread a darning needle with wool, first thread a loop of cotton through the eye and use this to draw the wool through.

If you have difficulty getting a needle through a stiff fabric, stroke the needle through your hair once or twice. The natural oils in your hair will lubricate it.

To sharpen a sewing machine needle, stitch for several inches through a piece of fine sandpaper, then hold a burning match to the tip for a minute or two.

To prevent sewing thread knotting, always thread the loose end through the needle, and knot the end that has been broken from the reel.

Oily machine

When you have oiled your sewing machine, sew through blotting paper for a few inches to avoid getting oil on fabric.

Second-hand zips

Spray an old zip with starch and it will come up like new. (Jumble sales are a good source of all sorts of second-hand sewing notions.)

Sewing fur

Instead of laboriously tacking seams together, use a stapler.

Thimbles

Don't buy porcelain thimbles. They are pretty but impractical: they won't stay on your finger.

Cookery

To be a good cook, you need first to be good at shopping so that you can choose the best, freshest ingredients. You need to know what fresh meat and fish look like. (Beef should be bright red; pork should be pale pink; English lamb is pink with creamy fat whereas the fat on New Zealand lamb is white; fresh fish will still have bright bulging eyes.) You need to know what's in season. Although this hardly applies to meat any longer, it does apply to fish (see page 142), game (page 142) and vegetables. Make friends with your local shopkeepers so that you can be sure of getting what you ask for. Then you can plan your menu while you shop.

It helps, of course, if you have a reliable repertoire of menus. For a potentially nerve-racking occasion, it is always wiser to make dishes you are familiar with. And remember, a meal can be impressive without being expensive. Be versatile: learn how to make all sorts of subtle vegetable soups, do delicious things with offal, and make simple, fruity desserts. Make the most of cheaper cuts of meat with pot roasts and slowly-simmering daubes. Make nourishing protein-rich soups and stews using dried peas and beans.

A 'good cook' is often judged on just one item: the crispness of chips, the fluffiness of rice, the crunchiness of crackling, the height of Yorkshire pudding, the lightness of pastry. Make sure you pass all of these tests by taking the hints that follow.

Some general rules:

Use the best ingredients. Choose a good-quality oil for cooking: buy it in bulk to save money and store it carefully (page 90). If you use butter, choose a high-quality brand. Whenever possible, use fresh herbs and don't keep dried ones for more than a month or two, or they lose all flavour.

Get to know about food values so you can plan balanced, nutritious meals.

Master basic techniques. Do you know the most efficient way to chop an onion (page 73), stone a cherry (page 85), de-rind bacon (page 75)?

Use the best utensils and look after them. It's worth paying more for heavy iron pans which will protect food from burning and seal all the flavour in. Use French carbon steel cooks' knives, and clean and sharpen them regularly.

Vegetables

Blanching

Blanching preserves the freshness and colour of green

vegetables. Bring to the boil a large saucepanful of salted water – approximately six pints (3 litres) for every pound (500 g) of vegetables. Drop the vegetables in and bring back to the boil.

If they are to be eaten at once, continue simmering until the vegetables are tender but firm. If not, remove them from the boiling water after a minute or two and plunge them into a large bowl of cold water. Leave for a few minutes, then remove and drain.

Boiling

To stop vegetables boiling over, add a small piece of butter or another fat to the pan.

All vegetables that grow above ground (i.e. green ones) should be boiled with the saucepan lid off. All those that grow below ground (i.e. root vegetables) should be boiled with the lid on.

Steaming

Steam green vegetables to preserve all their vitamins. Use a colander placed over a pan of boiling water and covered with the lid.

Aubergines

Aubergines should always be sliced, tossed with salt and left to drain for half an hour to let their bitter juices escape before cooking. Wipe dry with a clean cloth or kitchen towel.

Celery

Cut off the leafy tops of celery, dry them in a slow oven and use to flavour soups and stews.

Lettuce

To revive a limp lettuce, wash it well, shake it, wrap it in a clean cloth and place in the refrigerator (or an aluminium saucepan with the lid on) for an hour.

Or, soak the lettuce for half an hour in a bowl of cold water with a teaspoonful of sugar dissolved in it.

If you haven't got a salad shaker, wrap washed lettuce in a muslin bag and swing vigorously back and forth to throw off the water.

Onions

If you peel and chop onions under water they won't make you cry.

When dicing an onion leave the stem on to hold it together. First slice the onion in half from top to bottom, and lay the flat surface on the chopping board. Make vertical cuts, then horizontal cuts, then vertical cuts at right angles to the first ones.

Potatoes

Keep a wire pan-scourer specially for scraping new potatoes. It will remove the skin easily and leave you the vitamins that are just beneath it.

Light and creamy mashed potatoes can be made by draining the cooked potatoes, drying them off in the saucepan over a low heat, then breaking them up with a fork, making a well in the centre and adding the required amount of milk and butter. Wait until the milk starts to boil, then beat vigorously.

For particularly crisp chips, sprinkle cut chips with salt and wrap them in a clean tea towel (specially reserved for this purpose) for ten minutes before cooking them in very hot oil or fat.

Spinach

There is no need to add water when cooking spinach. After you have washed it (in several changes of water) enough moisture will cling to the leaves for it to be cooked in.

Tomatoes

Cover tomatoes with very hot water for a minute or two and they will be easy to peel.

Add a pinch of sugar when cooking tomatoes, to counteract their bitterness. A pinch of sugar will also bring out the natural sweetness of carrots and turnips.

Herbs

Rather than using a chopping board and knife, it is easier and more efficient to chop fresh herbs into a cup with sharp kitchen scissors.

To make your own bouquet garni, tie together two sprigs of parsley, one bay leaf and a sprig of thyme. If you use dried herbs, wrap them in a piece of muslin.

Pasta and rice

Pasta

Always cook pasta in a large saucepan with plenty of salted water. A teaspoon of oil added to the water will stop it sticking together.

A good test of whether spaghetti is cooked is to throw a strand at the wall. If it is ready it will stick there.

Three ways of cooking perfect rice for four people

1. Heat oven to gas mark 5, 375°F, 190°C. Bring to the boil a large saucepanful of salted water, and tip in two cups of long-grain rice. Bring back to the boil, stirring occasionally, and simmer for eight minutes. Strain and rinse under hot running water. Transfer to an oven-proof dish and place in the oven for five minutes. Fluff with a fork.

2. Heat oven to gas mark 5, 375°F, 190°C. Put two cups of rice in a lidded casserole with five cups of boiling water. Add salt to taste, cover and place in the oven for exactly half an hour.

3. Sauté two cups of rice in a tablespoon of oil or butter until transparent. Then add four cups of cold water with salt to taste, cover, bring to the boil and simmer very gently for about twelve minutes.

Meat and dairy products

Bacon

It is quicker to cut off bacon rinds with sharp scissors than with a knife.

Or, nick the end of the rasher and simply pull the rind off.

To clarify butter

Clarified butter is a wonderful medium for crisp, light frying. It can be heated to a very high temperature without burning. To make it, heat butter gently in a heavy pan to just below simmering point, and maintain this temperature for up to forty-five minutes, until much of the moisture has evaporated and the impurities have collected in the bottom of the pan. Strain the clear liquid carefully through muslin into an earthenware or stone container. Clarified butter will keep for up to a year in a cool place.

To clarify dripping

Pour boiling water over dripping in a pan, heat until completely melted, then leave to cool. A solid layer of pure dripping will form on top of the water. Remove this to keep, and pour off the water which contains all the impurities.

To coat with flour

To save mess – and washing up – when you need to coat pieces of meat or fish with flour, shake them with the flour in a paper bag. Old flour bags are even better.

Crackling

For particularly crisp crackling, score the skin of your joint of pork deeply, then brush with oil and rub with salt.

Cream

Cream should never be allowed to boil, or it will curdle. Add it to a hot dish just before serving and re-heat gently.

Add a teaspoon of lemon juice to a small carton of fresh double cream to make it 'sour'.

A few drops of lemon juice added to cream make it easier to whip.

Deep frying

A tablespoon of vinegar added to the fat before deep frying will stop food absorbing too much fat.

Evaporated milk

Add the juice of half a lemon to a small tin of evaporated milk and it can be whipped until stiff.

Marinate to slim

Meat marinated in lemon juice or vinegar is good for slimmers because these acids dissolve animal fats. Discard the marinade before cooking the meat.

Milk

To prevent milk (or porridge) boiling over, add a marble to the pan. This effectively stirs the contents. Remember to remove the marble before serving.

To pluck poultry

Immerse the bird in boiling water for one minute to make the plucking easier and stop the feathers flying.

To purify fat

To remove strong flavours from a pan of fat, slice a couple of raw potatoes into it and fry until brown. Remove them with a perforated spoon and strain the fat through a piece of muslin laid in a colander.

Sausages

So that sausages do not split when grilled or fried, first cover them with cold water in a saucepan, bring to the boil and drain.

Seasoned flour

For every eight ounces (250 g) of plain flour, add one level tablespoon of salt and a quarter of a tablespoon of pepper.

To skim fat from soup

A quicker way of removing excessive fat from soup, stock or gravy than skimming it off with a spoon is to pour it while hot through a cloth soaked in cold water. The grease will cling to the cloth.

Or, drop ice cubes into the pot. Fat will immediately cling to them, and they can be removed before they melt.

To tenderize meat

Vinegar makes meat tender. Rub a tough steak with a mixture of vinegar and oil and leave for two hours before grilling. Soak an old fowl in vinegar for several hours before roasting.

If you haven't got a meat mallet, use a rolling pin instead.

To truss poultry

Use dental floss.

Eggs

To separate an egg, crack it gently on to a saucer, hold the yolk in place with an egg cup, and drain off the white.

If you need to boil a cracked egg, add salt or vinegar to the water to stop the white coming out.

If you have no egg poacher, poach eggs in a pan of boiling water to which a teaspoonful of vinegar has been added.

If an egg has broken in a cardboard egg box and is difficult to remove, dip the box in water.

There is no difference in taste or food value between a brown egg and a white one.

In order to prevent dark rings forming around the yolks of hard-boiled eggs, take the eggs out of the pan as soon as they are cooked, crack the shells slightly and run cold water on to them until they are cool.

A knife repeatedly dipped in boiling water will slice hard-boiled eggs without making them crumble.

To prevent an omelette (or any other fried food) sticking to the pan, sprinkle salt into the pan and heat for a few seconds before using.

Bread and puddings

A knife repeatedly dipped in boiling water will cut soft new bread.

Breadcrumbs

If you have too much fresh bread, grate some to make breadcrumbs. Stored in a polythene bag in the refrigerator they will keep for a week or more, and can be used for making puddings.

Bread sauce without breadcrumbs

Cut white bread into small cubes and leave to dry for a couple of hours. Add to hot milk instead of breadcrumbs.

To make bread rise faster

When making a large loaf in a hurry, add a quarter of a teaspoon or one tablet of citric acid to the yeast mixture before combining it with the flour, and the bread will rise much faster. But be careful not to add any more than this!

Crumpets

Always toast the bottom of a crumpet first, so that the top is hotter when served and absorbs more butter.

To crush biscuits

To make biscuit crumbs for pudding bases, place the biscuits on a flat surface between greaseproof paper, with a clean tea towel folded above and below the paper. Alternatively, put the biscuits into a clean polythene bag. Roll firmly with a rolling pin.

Gelatine

Gelatine should always be dissolved in a little cold water before being added to other ingredients.

Jelly

To make jelly set more quickly, melt the cubes in only a small amount of hot water and make up the rest with cold water and ice cubes.

Wet the inside of the mould before pouring in the jelly and it will be easier to turn out.

Meringues

A pinch of cream of tartar added to the egg whites before whipping ensures that meringues will be crisp and dry. Add the caster sugar only a teaspoonful at a time, beating thoroughly in between additions. Cook very slowly (gas mark $\frac{1}{4}$, 225°F or 110°C) for about two hours until the meringues are quite dry; then remove and cool on a wire tray.

Steaming puddings

To avoid the discomfort of handling a hot basin or cloth when steaming a pudding, use a chip pan and basket.

When steaming puddings or heating tins of food, add a squeeze of lemon juice to the water to prevent the saucepan turning black.

To test yeast

If you suspect that the yeast you are using for breadmaking may no longer be active, test it by adding a tablespoon of flour to the yeast-and-water mixture (before adding the salt and sugar). If nothing happens in fifteen minutes, you need some new yeast.

Yorkshire pudding

To make a successful Yorkshire pudding, use half milk and half water in the batter. Mix it well in advance and leave to stand. Heat the empty tin in the oven, then add fat and heat this until it is smoking before pouring in the batter.

Pastry making

The secret of successful pastry making is coolness: hands, fat, water and rolling surface should all be as cold as possible. The marble top of an old wash-stand makes an ideal pastry board.

When rolling pastry, sprinkle flour on to your board and rolling pin, never directly on to the pastry.

Chill pastry in the refrigerator for half an hour before baking, and it will not shrink when cooked.

Keep a polythene bag beside you when making pastry so

you can slip a hand inside it to pick up the receiver if the phone rings.

To bake blind

In order to prepare a pastry case for a flan or tart, line the dish with the pastry, cover it with greaseproof or butter paper, and half fill with dried peas or beans (or uncooked rice). Bake for ten to fifteen minutes, until the pastry has set. Remove the peas and set them aside to cool (they can be stored in an airtight container and used again). Meanwhile add the filling and continue to cook as directed in the recipe.

Baked custards

Brush the pastry shell with egg white before adding the filling, to stop the custard getting underneath it.

Baking in glass

When baking pastry in glass ovenware, stand the container on a metal baking tray in the oven to make sure that the bottom crust is thoroughly cooked. (Glass is a poor conductor of heat.)

Cake making

Always prepare a cake tin by greasing it with butter paper and sprinkling with flour before pouring in the mixture. This will prevent the cake sticking.

If a cake does stick to the tin, stand the tin on a damp cloth for a few minutes after removing it from the oven.

Place a tray of water in the bottom of the oven while cakes are baking. The steam rising from this will stop the cakes burning.

If you open the oven door to look at cakes while they are baking, always close it gently afterwards. Any sudden or violent movement may make the cakes sink.

Egg substitute

If you run out of eggs, a tablespoon of vinegar may be substituted for one egg.

Fruit cakes

Before using dried fruit for baking, soak it in hot water, or steam it to make it soften and swell. Then dry it carefully, spread on a cloth in a warm place. (If you use it wet, it will make your cake sink.)

Use a wet knife to chop dried fruit and it will not stick to the blade.

Shake dried fruit in a paper bag containing a little flour before adding it to a cake mixture. This ensures that it will be evenly distributed through the cake.

Spread a thin layer of plain mixture in the bottom of the tin, and another on top of the fruity mixture. This gives a smooth surface, and prevents the fruit from burning.

Lemon-flavoured sugar

When a recipe calls for lemon or orange juice but not rind, grate off the rind anyway and store it in an airtight jar mixed with caster sugar. It will add a delicious flavour to Victoria sponges, shortbreads, etc.

Self-raising flour

If you run out of self-raising flour while baking, simply make your own by adding two and a half teaspoons (12·5 ml) of baking powder to half a pound (225 g) of plain flour.

Syrup

To prevent syrup sticking to the scales when being weighed, dust the scales first with flour.

Fruit and nuts

Acid fruit

A little lemon peel added to acid fruit such as rhubarb or apple counteracts their acidity and cuts down the amount of sugar required for sweetening.

Apples

Peel apples into a bowlful of salted water to prevent them going brown. When they are needed rinse thoroughly.

To blanch almonds

Pour boiling water over almonds in a basin and leave for five minutes. Drain. The skins will slip off easily.

Coffee made with a filter

The beans should be ground very finely. In order to get the full flavour of the coffee, add only a little boiling water at first, just enough to moisten all the coffee. When this has filtered through continue adding more water gradually.

Gooseberries

Use scissors to top and tail gooseberries.

Add a couple of medium-sized elderflower heads per pound (500g) of gooseberries when stewing to give them a delicious flavour and counteract acidity.

Prunes

For delicious prunes, soak overnight in cold tea, then stew in the same liquid until tender.

Rhubarb

Use scissors to chop rhubarb: it's quicker and doesn't pull off the skin.

To stone cherries

Insert the rounded end of a new hairpin in the stem end of the cherry, hook it around the stone and remove.

Strawberries

If you need to wash strawberries, do not hull them until afterwards, or they will go soft and mushy.

To test jam

To see if jam is done, drop a teaspoonful on to the bottom of an upturned ice-tray. If it is ready it will jell – more quickly than on a plate at room temperature.

Whole walnuts

To shell walnuts without breaking them, first soak overnight in salted water. Squeeze gently with nutcrackers.

Storage

Here are some simple, time-honoured ways of keeping food fresh – from lumps of sugar in the cheese dish to apples in the cake tin. Ways to keep everyday things like salt running freely and brown sugar soft. Ways too of storing things you don't get every day – from game to good wine.

You'll find that wardrobes don't need to smell of mothballs. There are all sorts of hints for making clothes smell sweet, with lavender bags (page 132), soap (page 40) or pomanders (page 94).

Some general hints:

Labels. You may think, as you tip that spice into a plain glass jar, that you will remember what it is – but you won't. And although *you* know what those various white powders are in the jars on the shelf, what if someone comes to stay?

Dates. Anything that is likely to deteriorate, particularly preserves and food you are freezing, should be dated. Spring-clean cupboards periodically. Throw away old medicines.

Warm or cool, light or dark, dry or moist, airy or airless? These are the questions you need to ask before putting *anything* into store.

Storing food

Apples

Store only unblemished apples. Place them on trays or racks, not touching one another, in a cool, airy place. Check them once a week and remove any that are not perfect.

Bottled fruit

Bottled fruit should be stored in a dark, well-ventilated cupboard. Light and warmth are liable to make the fruit ferment.

Bread

A glazed earthenware pot will keep bread moister longer.

Wash bread containers with a solution of one tablespoon vinegar to one pint (500 ml) of warm water to prevent mould forming.

Brown sugar

If soft brown sugar goes hard, empty it into a bowl, cover with a damp cloth, and leave overnight.

Cakes

A large cake will keep moist longer if you add a teaspoonful of glycerine to the mixture.

An apple placed in the cake tin will keep cake moist.

Carrots, turnips and beetroot

Harvest in October. Trim the tops and store in boxes between layers of sand or soil.

Cheese

Cheese should never be kept in a refrigerator. If you haven't got a cheese dish, wrap cheese in a piece of muslin moistened with vinegar and it will keep fresh. Moisten the cloth again as it dries out.

A sugar cube placed in the cheese dish prevents mould.

Cream crackers

Cream crackers will stay crisp if wrapped tightly in polythene and stored in the refrigerator.

Dried fruit

Never store dried fruit in tins, as the acid content of the fruit might cause corrosion.

Dried herbs

Hang freshly-picked herbs upside down in a paper bag.

When they are quite dry, rub them, still in the bag, between your hands. You will then have a bag of dried herbs ready for the storage jar, and no bits on the kitchen floor. Plastic bags are unsuitable because they do not allow the moisture from the herbs to evaporate, and the herbs tend to go mouldy.

Eggs

Eggs should always be stored at room temperature, and not in the refrigerator. The shells will not then crack when they are boiled, and mayonnaise made with them will not curdle.

Store eggs with the pointed end uppermost, and they will keep fresh longer.

If an egg rises to the surface of a bowl of cold water it is stale and should be thrown away.

Pour a little cold water over left-over egg yolks and they will keep in the refrigerator for several days.

Egg whites will keep for up to two weeks if stored in an airtight container in the refrigerator.

Freezing

Freeze soup and casseroles in square bread tins. When frozen, dip the base of the tin quickly in hot water to loosen the contents, remove, then wrap, label and return to freezer.

When freezing a large cake, cut it first into several pieces so that they can be defrosted one at a time, as required.

Spray ice cubes with soda from a syphon before putting them in a plastic bag in the freezer, and they will not stick together when removed.

Game birds

A freshly-killed bird should not be plucked or drawn, but hung up by the feet in a cool, dry, airy place. Allow four days for a partridge, a week for other birds in warm weather or two to three weeks in cold weather. Check regularly until the flesh begins to smell 'gamey'.

Garlic

Separate a head of garlic into cloves, peel each one and store in a small jar of olive oil. This will keep them moist and eventually you can use the oil for making garlic-flavoured salad dressing.

Jam

Save screw-top jars for jam-making. Seal the pots with wax circles and cellophane tops in the usual way when the jam is made but after it is opened, replace them with the original tops.

Lemons

To keep lemons fresh and juicy, store them in a bowl of water in a cool place.

Marrows

To keep vegetable marrows fresh, cover the cut stem with sealing wax.

Mustard

Cover left-over mustard with a little cold water and it will keep for several days.

Olive oil

Olive oil should not be allowed to get too warm or too cold. If it's too warm it will go rancid; too cold and it will go cloudy. If it goes rancid there's nothing you can do; if it goes cloudy you can warm it gently and it will clear.

Onions, shallots and garlic

Lift from the garden before the first frost. Tie the stems in bunches and hang in a dry, airy place.

Parsley

Fresh parsley will keep for at least two weeks in a refrigerator if either tightly wrapped in cling film or pressed down firmly (leaving no air space) in a screw-top jar.

Potatoes

Leave for six hours to dry in the open air after digging up, then store in boxes in a frost-proof, dark place.

To ripen pears

Both avocado and dessert pears can be ripened quickly in the airing cupboard or on a sunny window ledge.

Salads

Line the salad drawer of a refrigerator with paper towels to absorb excess moisture.

Salt

Keep salt running freely by adding a couple of dried peas or a few grains of rice to the salt cellar.

Tomatoes

Tomatoes can be picked when quite green, but should not then be ripened in direct sunlight (which would make them go soft). What they need is warmth: so place them on a tray on top of the fridge or freezer, or in the airing cupboard.

Storing other things

Coal

Coal should always be stored in darkness, or it tends to crumble.

Labels

If you write your own labels for kitchen storage jars, cover them with transparent sticky tape so that they do not get smudged.

Long dresses

Sew loops inside the waists of long dresses to hang them up by, so that they don't trail on the floor of the wardrobe.

Nail varnish

Keep nail varnish in the refrigerator and it will stay runny.

Old lace

Keep in a warm dry place to prevent mould forming. Take the lace out and air it from time to time.

Records

Records should always be stored vertically; if laid flat they are liable to warp.

Screws

To store different sized nails, screws, etc., conveniently, screw or nail the lids of suitable jars to the underside of an eye-level shelf. The jars themselves can then be screwed on to or off the lids when required. This arrangement can also be used for food.

Silver

Wrap silver and silver plate in plastic bags and store away from the light to keep them from tarnishing.

Silver teapots

Put two sugar lumps inside your silver teapot and store it with the lid open in an airy place to prevent it acquiring a stale smell.

Steel wool

Dissolve a teaspoonful of salt in a little hot water in a jar. Put a used (non-soapy) steel wool pad in it and it will keep indefinitely without going rusty.

String

Keep a ball of string in a screw-top jam jar with the end threaded through a hole punched in the lid. You'll never lose the end or find the string in a tangle.

Wine

Ideally wine should be stored at between 50°–60° F (10–15° C). But whatever the temperature, it must be kept constant.

Unlike spirits, bottles of wine should be stored lying down so that the wine remains in contact with the cork.

Wineglasses

Wineglasses should not be stored upside down: they are liable to develop a musty smell.

Woollens

Wrap woollen garments in newspaper to store during the summer: this will deter moths.

To make a pomander

>   1 small thin-skinned orange
>   fresh whole cloves
>   1 teaspoon powdered cinnamon
>   1 teaspoon powdered orris root

Stud the entire surface of the orange with cloves. If the tips are not sharp enough, use a bodkin to make holes for them; but do not pierce the orange deeply enough to make the juice run out.

Mix the cinnamon and orris root (or use cinnamon alone if you prefer) and roll the orange in the powder, rubbing and patting it well in. Wrap in greaseproof paper and leave for five to six weeks in a cool dry place.

Shake off any loose powder and the pomander is ready to use. Hang it up by a ribbon to perfume a wardrobe, or place in a linen cupboard or chest of drawers.

Stains

The vital requirements for stain removal are a well-stocked storecupboard (see page 11) and speed. Speed is essential: many marks can be removed using nothing more complicated than cold water, as long as you treat them immediately. If you delay, the staining agent may cause permanent damage.

Other basic principles are:

Treat stains before laundering. Many stains, particularly those caused by the proteins in food or body fluids, can be removed by soaking in cold water. Hot water will 'set' the proteins and make them impossible to remove.

Test the solvent first. Before attacking the stain with the appropriate solvent, apply a little of it first to an unobtrusive part of the stained article, to make sure that it is not going to damage it.

Approach stains from behind. Whenever possible encourage a stain to leave the way it came. Place the stained item face down on a clean absorbent cloth and apply the solvent from the reverse side.

Start from the outside. In order to avoid the 'tide mark' that is often left after stains have been treated, start applying the solvent at the outer edge and work inwards.

Stains on carpets and furniture

Ball-point pen ink

Sponge with dry-cleaning solvent, blot dry, then apply solution of one teaspoon of washing-up liquid in half a pint (250 ml) warm water. Rinse and blot dry.

Beer

Mop, then dab with a solution of one teaspoon of washing-up liquid in half a pint (250 ml) lukewarm water. Blot dry with a clean cloth.

Blood

Sponge with a solution of one teaspoon of washing-up liquid in half a pint (250 ml) lukewarm water. Blot dry, then sponge with clear cold water and dry again.

Cigarette burns

A cigarette burn on a carpet should be treated by first rubbing lightly with fine sandpaper to remove the charred fibres. Then drip a mild detergent solution (Stergene in water) on to the stain, cover with dry borax and rub in with the fingertips. Leave for five minutes and sponge with a damp cloth.

To treat polished wood which has been burned by a cigarette, rub gently with very fine steel wool, rub in a little linseed oil and leave for twenty-four hours. Then apply polish.

Coffee

Spray with a soda syphon, then sponge with a solution of washing-up liquid in water. Blot dry.

Felt-tip pen ink

It is virtually impossible to remove these stains: it's wise to leave them alone rather than risk making them worse. Better still, use the new kind of felt-tip pens whose ink is water-soluble.

Fountain pen ink

While the ink is still wet, cover thickly with salt. Scrape up with a spoon as it becomes discoloured, and repeat. When no more ink is absorbed, rub the spot with a cut lemon and rinse with clear water.

You may be able to remove dry stains with a washing-up liquid solution, as for ball-point pen ink; or they may need to be treated professionally.

Grease

Treat immediately. Blot first with blotting paper or kitchen towels. If the mark is still visible sprinkle it with talcum powder, coarse salt or oatmeal. Leave for as long as possible, then vacuum or brush.

If the grease has been allowed to dry, mix a paste of oatmeal or salt with dry-cleaning solvent. Apply this to the stain, leave for an hour, then vacuum or brush.

Grease on wood

If grease is spilt on a wooden floor or table, pour cold water over it at once to make the fat congeal before it can penetrate the wood. Scrape up as much as possible with a knife.

Varnished surfaces may then be sponged with warm soapy water containing a spoonful of white spirit.

Or, make a paste of fuller's earth, soap and water, apply this to the stain and leave for a day or two.

Unvarnished surfaces should be washed with a strong solution of washing soda in warm water.

Ink on unvarnished wood

Unvarnished surfaces should be sponged with white spirit. Allow to dry, then wash with clear water.

Milk and cream

Sponge with a solution of one teaspoon of washing-up liquid in half a pint (250 ml) lukewarm water.

Mud

Sprinkle salt on muddy footprints at once. Leave for half an hour, then vacuum. This also works for soot and tea.

Red wine

To remove red wine stains from a carpet, sprinkle liberally

with salt, leave for a few minutes or until the salt has absorbed all the colour of the wine, and remove with lots of cold water.

Alternatively, spray with a soda syphon then sponge with clear water.

Dried stains may be treated with a solution of equal parts of glycerine (or hydrogen peroxide) and warm water. Leave for a quarter of an hour, then sponge or rinse.

Ring marks on French polish

Combine six parts methylated spirit with two parts linseed oil and a few drops of pure turpentine. Rub this into the mark with a soft cloth, then polish as usual.

Or, rub gently with a very fine steel wool pad (to lift the polish and smooth the wood grain) and then restore the surface with an ordinary furniture polish.

Or, dip a cloth into the clear liquid that collects on the top of a tin of brass cleaner, rub this in gently, and polish.

Tea

See Mud (page 98).

Urine

If puppies, kittens or babies make puddles on your carpet, spray the affected area with soda from a soda syphon. (Bottled soda does not work.) Leave to soak in, then sponge.

Vomit

Mop up with a damp cloth, then spray on soda from a syphon to get rid of the smell.

Stains on fabrics

Acids

Rinse with plenty of cold water, then neutralize with a solution of household ammonia or bicarbonate of soda.

Adhesives

Cellulose-based household adhesive, modelling cement, and contact adhesive stains can be removed with acetone or non-oily nail varnish remover. Do not use this, however, on acetate fabrics.

Ball-point pen ink

Treat immediately. Dab with a little methylated spirit or acetone.

Beer

Dab with white vinegar, then rinse. If the stain persists, soak with biological washing powder.

Beetroot

Soak in a solution of a tablespoon of borax to a pint (500 ml) of warm water.

Biological washing powder

The enzymes in biological washing powder break down proteins during soaking, which means they can be used to remove stains caused by body proteins in blood, urine, semen and sweat, as well as food proteins in, for example, eggs. This is a slow process: soak overnight in cool or lukewarm water.

Blood

Treat while still wet. Dip in cold water, sprinkle on plenty of salt, leave for twelve hours and rinse.

If the stain has dried, soak in biological washing powder solution for twelve hours.

Candle wax

To remove candle wax from fabric, place non-waxed brown paper under and over the mark and press gently with a hot iron.

Carbon paper

Stains on non-washable fabrics should be dabbed with methylated spirit. On washable fabrics use a little household ammonia, then neat washing-up liquid. Rinse thoroughly.

Chewing gum

If you get chewing gum stuck to your clothes, freeze the fabric (by pressing an ice cube wrapped in a plastic bag against it) so that you can crack the gum off, and then remove the residue by covering with brown paper and ironing it.

Chocolate

Rub the stain vigorously with glycerine, leave for ten minutes, then wash in lukewarm water.

Cocoa

Soak in cold water, then dip the stain in boiling water containing borax. Alternatively pour boiling water through the stain.

Coffee

Sponge with warm soapy water and leave to dry. If stain persists, dab with dry-cleaning solvent.

Crayon

Apply dry-cleaning solvent, then sponge with methylated spirit.

Creosote

Sponge with eucalyptus oil.

Egg stains

Soak in cold clear water before washing in hot soapy water.

Emulsion paint

While it is still wet emulsion paint can be removed by rinsing in cold water. If the stain has dried use methylated spirit, several times if necessary.

Engine oil

Use neat washing-up liquid. This works for hands, too.

Epoxy resin adhesive

Epoxy resin adhesive, as used for repairing china, can be removed with methylated spirit – but only before it sets.

Fruit juice on delicate fabrics

Sponge with surgical spirit containing a few drops of household ammonia.

Fruit juice on washable fabrics

If treated promptly, fruit stains on washable fabrics can be removed by stretching the stained article across a large bowl and pouring boiling water through the stain. Alternatively, rub with a solution of cream of tartar before washing in the usual way.

Stains which have been allowed to dry may be removed by applying glycerine first. Leave for an hour, then pour boiling water through the stain.

Gloss paint

Dab with white spirit.

Glue

Animal or fish glue stains on washable fabrics can be removed by soaking in hot water and white vinegar. Non-washable fabrics should be sponged with a vinegar-water solution.

Grass

Sponge with warm soapy water and a little methylated spirit, or with eucalyptus oil.

Grease

Washable fabrics may be soaked in a weak washing soda solution (a few crystals per bowlful of warm water). Or, use a solution of household ammonia made up according to the instructions on the bottle.

Non-washable fabrics may be treated with a borax solution – one teaspoonful per half pint (250 ml) of warm water.

Indian ink

Stains can be removed by sponging with surgical spirit.

Ink on non-washable fabrics

Rinse out as much as possible by sponging with cold, clear water, then cover the mark with salt, wet it with lemon juice, and lay it in the sun to dry.

Or, cover with a thick paste of milk and starch. Leave this for two days, then brush it off, and sponge with clear water.

Ink on washable fabrics

Soak the stain in milk for two or three days, until the milk turns sour. Alternatively, soak in tomato juice.

Lipstick

Sponge with methylated spirit, then with neat washing-up liquid. Rinse thoroughly.

Make-up

Apply a dry-cleaning solvent, then soap and water.

Mascara

Sponge with washing-up liquid, then with household ammonia. Rinse well.

Mildew

Brush, then apply hydrogen peroxide, then rinse.

Or, rub with a paste made of two teaspoons of salt, one teaspoon of starch and a few drops of lemon juice. Leave to dry (outside if possible) for several hours, then wash.

Milk or cream

Washable fabrics should be soaked in a strong borax solution, then washed in cold soapy water followed by warm.

Perfume

Sponge with neat household ammonia, then washing-up liquid. Rinse thoroughly.

Perspiration

Two aspirin tablets dissolved in the water will help to wash out perspiration stains.

Non-washable fabrics may be treated by dabbing with a solution of one tablespoon of vinegar in a quarter of a pint (150 ml) of warm water.

Plasticine

Scrape off as much of the plasticine as you can with a blunt knife, then dab the mark with lighter fuel.

Printer's ink

Sponge with white spirit or methylated spirit.

Rust or iron mould

Rub with lemon juice or citric acid and salt. This also works for mildew.

Scorch marks on fabric

Add a tablespoon of borax to a pint (500 ml) of warm soapy water and sponge the mark with this. Then gently rub in a little glycerine with the fingertips. Leave for a few minutes, then rinse in several changes of warm water.

Shellac

Apply methylated spirit, then rinse.

Shoe polish

Sponge with a dry-cleaning solvent, then a mixture of washing-up liquid and household ammonia. Rinse.

Soda

Stains from alkali such as washing, baking and caustic soda should be rinsed immediately with plenty of cold water and then neutralized with white vinegar.

Spirits

First try washing in cold water, but if this does not work sponge with methylated spirit.

Tar

Eucalyptus oil will remove beach tar from feet, shoes and clothing.

Tea

Sponge immediately with borax and warm water (one tablespoon of borax to half a pint – 250 ml – warm water).

Tide marks

As an extra precaution against the tide mark which is liable to remain after a stain has been removed, sprinkle the whole area (on the right side) with baby powder while still damp. Cover with a dry cloth, then iron dry.

Urine

Wash in warm water, then sponge with a solution of one tablespoon vinegar to one pint (500 ml) of water.

Vomit

Sponge with a solution of borax – one teaspoonful per pint (500 ml) of warm water.

Stains elsewhere

Grease on leather

Sponge with surgical spirit.

Grease on paper

Lay a piece of blotting paper over the spot and press with a warm iron. If this does not entirely remove the mark, cover thickly with fuller's earth and leave for twenty-four hours.

Grease on suede

Sponge with white vinegar, then brush with a suede brush.

Label marks

To remove the remains of stick-on labels from glass, plastic or china, rub on a little acetone or non-oily nail varnish remover, then wipe with a damp cloth. Alternatively, rub with white spirit.

Silver

Remove egg stains from silver cutlery by rubbing with salt on a damp cloth.

Or, dip in hot water in which potatoes have been boiled.

Sticky plaster

Traces of sticky plaster can be removed from the skin with eucalyptus oil or lemon juice.

Laundry

In this section you'll find some fascinating tips about making your own starch and blanket shampoo; advice on how to molly-coddle feather pillows, candlewick bedspreads, embroidery, velvet, jumpers and smalls so that they come up like new; and labour-saving ways of cleaning collars, pressing trousers and washing net curtains.

But the common theme of all of this advice is: proceed with caution. If you're laundering a new article, or an old one that isn't labelled with washing instructions; if it's likely to shrink; if the colours may run; if the fabric is particularly delicate – then DON'T put it in the washing machine, DON'T use hot water, DON'T use harsh detergents. If you've ever had a favourite garment come out of the wash transformed beyond recognition because these rules weren't followed – and had that awful helpless feeling because there's nothing you can do about it – then you won't need this warning.

Some general rules:

Always read the washing instructions, which by law all new garments must have. If you make your own clothes, find out the correct laundering procedure when you buy the fabric. Familiarize yourself with both old and new fabrics, so that you can cope with anything that isn't, for whatever reason, labelled.

Test first, for colour-fastness, for instance, dip an un-noticeable corner of the article in water and then press it between two pieces of white fabric with a warm iron. If colour comes out, wash the article very carefully, by itself.

If in doubt, dry-clean.

Airing cupboard

Freshly laundered linen should be placed at the bottom of the pile so that things are used in rotation.

Blankets

Blankets should be washed before being put away for the summer. If they are machine-washable, follow manufacturer's instruction for a gentle washing cycle. If you prefer to wash them by hand, use this shampoo.

Stir together eight ounces (250 g) soap flakes, a breakfastcupful of methylated spirit and three dessertspoonfuls of eucalyptus oil. When the mixture is smooth and creamy add a tablespoonful to each gallon (4 litres) of warm water. No rinsing is required. This treatment will help to keep moths away. Store the shampoo in a lidded jar.

Bleaching

To whiten cotton or linen, add one tablespoon of household chlorine bleach to two gallons (8 litres) of cold water. Soak the article in this mixture for fifteen minutes, then rinse well before washing in the usual way.

To whiten wool that has yellowed, mix one part hydrogen peroxide with eight parts cold water and soak the garment in this for up to twelve hours. Rinse, then wash.

Collars

Brush shampoo into collars to remove rings of dirt.

Corduroy

Corduroy and crepe should always be ironed gently on the wrong side using a damp cloth.

Cotton

Remove the dressing from new cotton or linen articles before washing by soaking in cold salted water.

Drying

Keep an old towel specially for rolling delicate fabrics like woollens and silks in after washing.

Lightweight jumpers can be hung up to dry without spoiling their shape by threading a stocking through the sleeves and attaching this to the clothes line.

To dry a candlewick bedspread, fold it over the line with

the fluffy surface inside. As it blows in the wind the friction will brush up the pile.

Embroidery

Lay the embroidery face down on a thick towel and iron the back.

Face cloths

If face cloths get slimy, boil in vinegar and water (a teaspoonful to one pint or 500 ml) for ten minutes.

Feather pillows

Dissolve a handful of soap flakes in a bathful of warm water, place feather pillows in this and tread them with bare feet to coax out dirt. Repeat with fresh soapy water if necessary, then rinse thoroughly and hang out to dry. (This may take several days.)

Ironing

Use a plastic plant-sprayer for dampening laundry before ironing.

It is more efficient to iron delicate fabrics – those which require a cool iron – first, and gradually raise the temperature as you proceed.

Freshly ironed clothes which are still warm and perhaps damp from ironing will crease very easily, so they should not be worn or packed immediately.

Leather buckles

Always remove from clothes before dry cleaning or, alternatively, cover the buckles tightly with kitchen foil.

Mixed fibres

When washing, cleaning or ironing a fabric made from a mixture of fibres, use the treatment recommended for the most delicate fibre it contains.

Net curtains

To save ironing net curtains, fold them neatly and soak them, still folded, in hot soapy water. Rinse, still folded, then hang out to dry.

Or, when they are hanging on the line, thread a rod through the bottom hems.

Rinsing

It is essential to remove all the soap after washing. A simple rule when washing by hand is to go on rinsing in several changes of water until the water remains absolutely clear.

White vinegar helps to get soap out of laundry as well as hair. Add a tablespoon to the final rinsing water when washing by hand, and a cupful when using a washing machine.

If you put a handful of salt in the final rinsing water it will help to stop clothes freezing on the line on a winter's day.

Shirts

Iron the double thicknesses of material first – the collar and cuffs (wrong side first, then right side). Then iron the sleeves, pressing the underarm seam first so as to centre the top fold. Finally iron the body of the shirt, starting (if you are right-handed) from the right edge, with the collar to your left.

Smalls

To prevent them getting damaged or tangled in a washing

machine, put tights and underwear in a pillowcase (tied up with a shoe lace or tape) and wash on the 'warm' cycle.

Starch

For moderate stiffness, add a quarter of a cupful of starch to two pints (1 litre) of boiling water; half a cupful for a stiff finish. Mix the starch to a thin, smooth paste and stir slowly while pouring on the boiling water.

Home-made starch

Pour about a pint (500 ml) of boiling water on to two ounces (50 g) of powdered gum arabic. Cover and leave to set overnight. Next day decant into a screw-top jar to store.

Trouser creases

If you are nervous about pressing creases in the legs of trousers and jeans, tack loosely along the crease before washing them.

Trouser press

If no iron is available, press trousers overnight while you sleep. Moisten the front and back creases with a damp towel and lay the trousers under your underblanket. By morning the trousers will have been well ironed by the heat and weight of your body.

Velvet

Velvet should never be ironed, but steamed. Hang small items over the spout of a boiling kettle, large ones over a hot bath.

Household Pests and Problems

This is the chapter that will make you really popular with your friends. Read and digest all the hints that follow, and you'll be the kind of person everyone needs in an emergency. You'll know how to cope with the thorniest, the most ticklish, the smelliest and stickiest of problems, from the relatively hum-drum, like frozen pipes (page 123) and hangovers (page 123), to the rather more exotic, such as what to do with a warped record (page 125) and how to put a cork back into a bottle (page 117). You'll display a cool capacity for improvisation when it comes to de-misting icy wind-screens (page 123) and finding a gas leak (page 123), an impressive knowledge of folklore about keeping ants out of the pantry (page 116) and moths out of your drawers (page 117), and breathtaking ingenuity in taking tight rings off fingers (page 119) and clearing the air in smoky rooms (page 120). You'll become famous for knowing how to prevent problems as well as solve them. In fact your only problem will be that you won't get a minute's peace.

Ants

Draw a chalk line across the floor where ants come into the house, and they won't cross it any more.

Hang bunches of green sage in your pantry to keep red ants away.

Bees and wasps

If you are troubled by bees on a picnic or in the garden, place a jar half full of water with a little jam or beer added several yards away. The bees will be attracted to this rather than you, and will drown in it.

Flies

Bunches of fresh stinging nettles hung at the window will keep flies out of the house.

To keep flies away, mix half a teaspoonful of ground black pepper, a teaspoonful of brown sugar and a tablespoonful of cream. Leave out in a saucer, and flies will not come near.

Mice

Hang bunches of watercress in your larder to keep mice away.

Moths

When you buy a second-hand chest of drawers or wardrobe, dab household ammonia in the corners to kill moth eggs.

Instead of mothballs, hang in your wardrobe a stocking containing dried orange peel.

Sprinkle allspice berries into drawers to keep moths out of clothes.

If moths get into your carpet, go over the whole affected area with a hot iron, pressing with a cloth moistened with cold water. This will kill any eggs and larvae.

Woodworm

To kill woodworm, apply liquid paraffin with a small paint brush so that it gets into all the holes. Then melt some beeswax and spread this over the affected area. When it is dry rub down and polish.

Sticky problems

Bolts

To loosen a rusted bolt, apply a few drops of household ammonia.

Bottle tops

If a bottle top is firmly stuck and you can't unscrew it by holding it with a cloth, try gripping it with sandpaper.

Corks

If a cork swells and is too big for its bottle, soak it for a few minutes in boiling water. It will then be soft enough to squeeze to the required size.

Curtain rods

Rub silicon polish on metal curtain rods to make the runners move more freely.

Doors

If a door sticks, rub some chalk down the edge where it meets the frame. Close it, and the chalk will leave a mark on the frame showing where the door is sticking. It can then be sanded or planed.

Drawers

Rub a candle along the runners to ease awkward drawers.

Glasses

If two glasses get stuck together, pour cold water into the top one and stand the bottom one in hot water. After a minute or two they should come apart easily.

Irons

If your iron is not running smoothly, wrap a piece of soap in some cotton material and rub the iron several times over this while hot.

Ketchup

If hand cream, scouring cream, ketchup, etc. refuse to flow out of the bottle when it is first opened, insert a drinking straw to introduce air.

Lids

When a metal lid is hard to remove from a glass jar, hold it under a hot tap. The metal lid will expand faster than the glass, and be easy to take off.

Or, release the vacuum by inserting a tough spoon handle or similar object under the rim and pulling away from the jar.

Or, try nut crackers.

Rings

If a ring gets stuck on your finger, thread one end of a piece of strong fine thread between the ring and your finger and wind it several times round the finger as far as the first joint. Take the ring end and unwind it slowly upwards, using it as a lever to move the ring. Dental floss is ideal for doing this.

Sash windows

Rub sashes and runners occasionally with soap or a white wax candle: the windows will move more easily and the sashes will last twice as long.

Screws

If a screw is difficult to remove, apply a red-hot poker to the head. Alternatively, hold a screwdriver to it and give the end of the screwdriver a sharp tap with a hammer.

Stoppers

If a glass stopper is stuck, pour a little vegetable oil on to it, hold the bottle near heat and tap lightly all round the stopper.

Zips

Rub a soft lead pencil up and down on a zip while it is closed and it will run more smoothly.

Smelly problems

Bottles

Half-fill with cold water and a couple of teaspoons of dry mustard. Replace the top and shake well, then open and leave to stand overnight before rinsing thoroughly.

Chopping board

It isn't necessary to keep an extra chopping board for smelly foods: simply mark one side with a spot of paint and use this only for onions, garlic, etc.

Cigarette smoke

Stuff a string bag or hairnet with straw and hang it from the ceiling. It will absorb cigarette smoke.

Or, burn candles.

Cutlery

To remove the smell of fish, egg or onion from silver cutlery, add a few drops of household ammonia to the washing-up water.

Dustbins

Sprinkle a little borax or a lot of salt into the dustbin to counteract unpleasant smells.

Fishy smell

After cooking fish, empty left-over tea and tea leaves into the pan and leave for ten minutes before washing. This will get rid of the fishy smell.

Garlic breath

Chew some fresh parsley to take away the smell of garlic.

Hands

To get rid of the smell after chopping onions or garlic, rub a little dry mustard into your hands.

Onion smells

After chopping onions or garlic, wash the knife in *cold* water to get rid of the smell.

Paint

Stand a bowl of water, or a bowl of vinegar, or a peeled and cut onion in a newly-painted room overnight to remove the smell.

Miscellaneous problems

Blocked drain

To clear a blocked drain, pour a little washing soda down it (a handful dissolved in boiling water) and then a cupful of vinegar.

Blocked shower spray

Unscrew the shower rose and soak it in vinegar overnight.

Blunt scissors

Sharpen scissors by drawing the blades back and forth around the neck of a glass bottle as if you were trying to cut the top off.

Or, cut sandpaper.

Chimney on fire

Close all doors and windows, and pour salt on to the fire in the grate to extinguish it. The fumes given off will overpower the flames in the chimney.

Cistern anti-freeze

If you have an outside lavatory, or a very cold bathroom, add a couple of teaspoons of glycerine to the water in the cistern to prevent it freezing in winter.

Creaking floorboards

Screw the creaking board to the joist below it. (Look for the nails in the next board to find where the joist is. Or, if there is a gap between the boards, slide a knife along between them to locate the joist.)

Creaking hinges

Rub hinges with a soft lead pencil or petroleum jelly and they will stop creaking.

Curdled mayonnaise

Put a teaspoon of the curdled mayonnaise into a clean, slightly warmed mixing bowl together with a teaspoon of made mustard. Beat together with a wire whisk until the mixture thickens, then add another teaspoon of mayonnaise and repeat. This method is infallible as long as you add the mayonnaise very slowly at first and beat thoroughly between additions.

Frozen lock

To prevent the lock on a car door from freezing in cold weather, cover it with sticky tape.

Frozen pipes

Frozen pipes should be thawed as quickly as possible. (Damage is done by water freezing and expanding, not by thawing. It is only by thawing the ice that you will find out if it has cracked the pipe.)

Turn the water off at the mains. Turn the tap on and, if the frozen pipe is indoors, aim a hairdryer at it. If it is out of doors, pour kettles of boiling water around it. If no leaks appear, turn on again at the mains.

Gas leak

In order to find a gas leak, coat the pipes, in the area where you suspect the leak is, with soapy water. The leak will blow bubbles.

As a temporary measure, until the gas man comes, plug the leak with a piece of soap.

Hangover

You need a prairie oyster. Break an egg into a glass, and add salt, pepper, Worcester sauce and vinegar to taste. Swallow in one gulp.

Icy windscreens

Rub with a cut potato or apple to prevent misting and icing.

Laddered tights

A blob of clear nail varnish will invisibly stop a ladder in an emergency.

Pipes

In very cold weather keep the plugs in baths, washbasins and sinks when not in use, so that drips do not make the waste-pipes freeze.

Saltiness

If a soup or stew is over-salty, add a raw peeled potato and continue simmering until the potato is tender. Remove it, and you will find it has absorbed much of the saltiness.

Scratched furniture

Scratches in polished wood can be treated with cod liver oil. Pour on to the scratch, leave until completely absorbed, then polish as usual.

Scratched watch face

Remove fine scratches from the face of a wrist-watch by rubbing gently with liquid brass cleaner.

Slow fire

Make a fire draw by holding an open newspaper across the fireplace, leaving a gap of one or two inches at the bottom. Be careful not to let the paper be drawn up the chimney as this could cause a chimney fire.

Steamy windows

Rub a little glycerine over mirrors and kitchen and bathroom window panes and they will not get steamed up.

Tight shoes

Pack with wet newspaper and leave overnight.

Warped records

If a record has become warped, lay it flat between two sheets of glass and leave outside in the sun for a day.

Wet shoes

Stuff with dry crumpled newspaper; rub with saddle soap; dry away from direct heat; polish.

Gardening

In a well-ordered garden everything has its time and place. This chapter tells you what time of day to cut roses and what time of year to cut lavender, when to plant bean seeds and when to harvest garlic. It even tells you where to plant your marigolds in relation to your potatoes, where to plant your potatoes in relation to where you planted them last year, how to keep bees and butterflies in the garden and greenfly and rabbits out.

It includes some good old-fashioned tips about the herb

garden, revealing how useful – and delightful – herbs can be to the gardener, quite apart from their many uses around the house. And then there are all sorts of ingenious suggestions about seedlings, fertilizers and houseplants: little things that save time and money and help to keep your house and garden smelling sweet.

Aspidistras

Occasionally put cold tea around the roots of an aspidistra, to act as a fertilizer.

Clean and polish the leaves with a mixture of half milk and half water.

Or, polish with a little olive oil.

Avocado pear tree

Make a slit with a knife in an avocado pear stone and place it in a glass of water in a warm, sunny place. (If you wish you can suspend it half in and half out of the water with toothpicks stuck into it on either side – but this is not essential.) When it starts to sprout (which may take several weeks), plant it in compost.

Beans

Instead of buying beans to plant, save the last crop from one year to use as seed. Leave to dry in their pods, then remove and keep until they start sprouting in the spring.

Bird netting

Put inverted yoghurt pots over the tops of canes to hold netting clear of fruit or vegetables.

Home-made cloche

You need four wire coat hangers, a garden cane and polythene sheeting of the required size. Cut each of the coat hangers at one corner and open the horizontal bar to form a vertical leg. Attach two pairs at the 'neck' and stand in the ground where needed. Fix the cane between the two 'necks', stretch the sheeting over the hangers and staple or stitch it in place.

Individual cloche

Cover an old lampshade frame with polythene to make an individual cloche for rhubarb or a plant that needs nurturing.

Compost heap

If you can't be bothered to strain vegetable peelings (this is particularly tedious with new potato scrapings) pour the water and peelings together on to the compost heap. The water is good for it.

Cuttings

Cover cuttings in pots with a polythene bag to create a humid atmosphere. The bag can be supported by loops of wire.

Cut flowers

If you are arranging only a few flowers, you will find that an odd number of flowers makes a more graceful group than an even number.

When arranging flowers, cut off the lower leaves so that none is submerged in water. Otherwise they will rot and harm the flowers.

If the stems of cut flowers are not long enough, put some screwed up newspaper at the bottom of the vase.

Cut flowers which arrive looking chilled or tired should be stood in warm water until they revive.

Roses should be cut early in the day, before the dew has dried.

Woody stems, such as those of roses or chrysanthemums, should be crushed by hammering with a rolling pin or split at the ends before being arranged in a vase. This will help to make the flowers last longer.

Before arranging tulips, take a large darning needle and pierce the stems every two inches from just below the flower head to the bottom.

To keep cut flowers fresh, change the water every day; cut off a little of the stems every day; place a copper coin in the vase.

Cyclamens

Cyclamens should always be watered from below. Stand them in a bowl of water for an hour or so, then pour off any water that remains.

Drainage

Put a layer of broken crockery or small pebbles in the bottom of flowerpots, garden tubs and window boxes to ensure good drainage.

A piece of net curtain placed over this before soil or compost is added will prevent drainage holes from clogging.

Egg box seed pots

Use cardboard egg boxes to plant seeds in. When they start to sprout, cut up and plant complete with the 'cups' – these will disintegrate underground and fertilize the plants.

Eggshell fertilizer

Half-fill a jar with eggshells, fill up with water and leave for three to four weeks. Use the liquid then to feed houseplants.

Home-made fertilizer

Put fresh lawn cuttings into an old bucket or tank and fill up with water. When this ferments it will make a fine liquid manure.

Frost

Plants likely to be damaged by frost should be watered with cold water in the evening.

Garden ties

Use discarded tights to tie up large shrubs or fruit trees that need support.

Garden tools

Paint garden tools with a spot of luminous or brightly coloured paint to avoid losing them among the weeds.

To keep tools rust-free through the winter, oil them and stand them in a bucketful of sand.

Garlic

Home-grown garlic is bigger and stronger. Simply plant individual cloves: they will soon sprout green shoots above ground. The bulbs grow underground like onions. Garlic is traditionally planted on Christmas Day and harvested at Michaelmas (29 September).

Geraniums

Leave geraniums in their pots when planting in beds for the summer; then it is easier to bring them indoors for the winter.

Feed geraniums by emptying cold coffee grounds around the roots.

A hanging basket

At Easter time line a wire basket with sphagnum moss (which you can buy at a seed merchant's). Put an old saucer or small plate on top of the moss, then fill the basket with potting compost. Plant colourful flowers like petunias, and trailing ones like geraniums, lobelia or nasturtiums, and hang in your porch. Water the basket about once a week, ideally by suspending it in a bucket of water overnight.

Herb-drying calendar

May to June: lemon balm, parsley, tarragon
June to August: basil, lavender, borage, chamomile, hyssop, lime, marjoram, mint, rosemary, sage, stinging nettle, thyme
August to September: dandelion, dill, fennel, juniper, lemon verbena, lovage, mustard, orris, poppy, savory, sunflower
October: burdock, chicory

Houseplants

Turn plants round regularly so that they get sunlight on all sides. Never leave houseplants standing in water for a long time: always allow to drain after watering.

Do-it-yourself houseplants

Pips from lemons, dates, passion fruit, persimmons, etc.,

planted in pots and kept warm and damp, will grow into unusual plants.

Lavender

Cut lavender in the first half of July (before St Swithin's Day, the 15th). Place in newspaper and dry in the airing cupboard for four days. Shake off the flowers and use to make lavender bags for drawers, or pot pourri (page 133). Tie the stems into bundles and use them to give a sweet perfume to winter fires.

Marigolds

Marigolds keep pests away from potatoes and tomatoes; grow them close together.

Mildew

Spray undiluted methylated spirit on to cabbages and sprouts to prevent mildew.

Milk for plants

Rinse milk bottles in cold water and pour this on to houseplants or into window boxes.

Motor mower

If your motor mower refuses to start, take out the plug and dip the sparking end in petrol. Replace, connect and the motor will start.

Newspaper fertilizer

Lay wet newspaper along the bottom of the trench when planting peas or beans. Sprinkle soil on top of it, then the seeds.

Patchy lawns

Add a few drops of detergent to a can of water and pour this on to brown dry patches. The detergent will help water to soak into the soil.

Picking sprouts

Pick sprouts from the bottom of the stem first: these are the ones that ripen first.

Planting small seeds

Before sowing small seeds, mix them with sand. Water the drills well, then sprinkle the mixture in. There is no need to cover with soil.

Plants from the north

It is a good policy when ordering plants by post to get them from a nursery to the north of where you live, so that the plants are coming to a more favourable southerly home.

Pot pourri

You will need:

the petals of three dozen roses
a handful each of the scented petals of flowers such as lavender, rosemary, carnation, acacia, jasmin, orange blossom, etc.
a handful each of the scented leaves of, for example, scented geranium, lemon verbena, mint, bay, balm, etc.
brightly coloured petals such as blue larkspur, marigold, etc.
a few pieces of angelica, washed, sliced and dried
a few pieces of orange or lemon rind
4 oz (100 g) powdered orris root

1 oz (25 g) coriander seed (optional)
1 oz (25 g) grated nutmeg
1 oz (25 g) whole cloves
2 or 3 sticks of cinnamon
½ oz (15 g) oil of geranium
½ oz (15 g) oil of lavender (optional)
a little allspice, mace and musk (all optional)
4 oz (100 g) salt

Pick the roses on a dry day, after the dew has evaporated. Spread the petals out on paper and leave them in a warm airy place, turning them frequently, until they are completely dry. Put them with the salt in a pottery or glass container with a well-fitting lid, cover and leave for five days, stirring twice daily.

Meanwhile pick and dry separately the other scented petals and leaves. At the end of the five days combine them with the rose petals.

Mix the oils with half the powdered orris root, then add the remaining ingredients. Stir them all into the dried flowers, cover and leave for three to four weeks, stirring occasionally.

If the mixture seems too moist add more orris; if too dry, more salt. Put the pot pourri into small bowls with pierced lids, and stir from time to time to release its perfume. Or put it in sachets to use like lavender bags.

Potting soil

The freshly-dug, aerated soil from molehills is ideal for potting houseplants.

To preserve flowers

Sprinkle generously with borax and leave in a dry place for two to three weeks. Keep in an airtight container.

Rain water

Rain water is better for plants than tap water. Stand jugs outside to collect it for watering houseplants, or collect it in a large butt for watering the garden.

Roses

Empty a teapot occasionally round the roots of rose bushes: it's good for them. Roses also thrive when fed with the muddy debris that collects in gutterings.

Strawberries

Slip clusters of ripening strawberries gently into glass jars lying on their sides. This will protect them from birds and make them ripen more quickly.

Sunshine

Plant rows of seeds running from north to south, so that one row of plants will not keep another in the shade.

Tomato pots

Old handleless or leaking plastic buckets are ideal for growing greenhouse tomatoes in.

Transplanting

If for some reason you have to move plants when it is very cold, use hot instead of cold water to puddle them in.

Vegetable crop rotation

For healthy crops, divide your vegetable garden into three plots. In year one, grow cabbages, brussels sprouts, cauliflowers, broccoli, etc., in the first plot; celery, potatoes, turnips, carrots and other root vegetables in the second; and peas, beans, leeks, lettuces and onions in the third. The next year grow the first group of vegetables in the second plot, the second group in the third plot, and the third group in the first plot. Rotate again in the third year, and in the fourth year start again.

To water plants in your absence

Place the end of a length of wool in a large jug of water, with the other end in the plant pot. The water will slowly be absorbed into the soil.

To water tomatoes, marrows or courgettes

Sink a flower pot into the ground near to each plant and pour water into this to keep the roots moist.

Window boxes and tubs

To save buying so much potting compost for tubs and window boxes, fill the bottom third of the container with vermiculite. It is cheaper and retains moisture so that less watering is necessary.

Home-made window boxes

Make your own window box with old floorboards nailed together. Drill holes at frequent intervals in the base. Paint the inside with non-toxic preservative, and outside with weatherproof paint.

Winter flower decorations

Save the dead flowerheads of hydrangeas, hang them up to

dry and then spray with silver or gold paint.

During the autumn, when beech leaves are at their most brilliant, cut some branches to keep. Stand them in a couple of inches of a mixture of half glycerine, half water. When all of this liquid has been absorbed, the branches can be arranged in a dry vase to make a decoration that will last through the winter.

Pick honesty during the autumn when the seed-containers have turned white, then carefully peel the outer coating from both sides of each one to leave only the translucent silvery centre.

Pick teasels and grasses to use in winter flower arrangements. Hang them upside down to dry in an airy place.

Wood ash for vegetables

Feed growing vegetables by spreading wood ash around their roots.

Weeds and animals

Ants

Ants are a pest in the garden: pour boiling water into anthills to destroy them.

Bees

To attract bees to your garden, whether to make honey or to help with pollination, grow the following: basil, bergamot, blackthorn, borage, catmint, golden rod, hawthorn, hollyhock, hyssop, lavender, marigold, marjoram, mint, poppy, sage, savory, sunflower, thyme, willow.

Butterflies

If you want butterflies in your garden, plant a buddleia (Butterfly Bush, or *Buddleia davidii*).

Earwigs

Dip lengths of string or wool in oil and tie them around the stems of dahlias and the sticks supporting them, about a foot (30 cm) above ground level. This will stop earwigs climbing up to the flowers.

Greenfly

Plant a row of parsley or garlic next to roses to keep greenfly away.

Herbal pesticide

To protect plants against pests, particularly aphids, spray with a herbal 'tea' made by pouring two pints (1 litre) of boiling water over two handfuls of fresh stinging nettles (or basil, or four crushed garlic cloves).

Or, simmer half a pound (225 g) of rhubarb or elder leaves for half an hour in a pint (500 ml) of water. Dilute before using with two more pints (1 litre) of cold water.

Rabbits

Place a few jam jars and wine bottles upside down among your vegetable plants. This will confuse rabbits and stop them eating your crop.

Slugs

Slugs can be trapped under an upturned grapefruit rind.

To kill slugs, sprinkle salt on them.

Or, set a jam jar containing a little beer in the ground near to plants that they like.

Snail trap

If snails are eating your plants, spread a little bran on the ground and cover it with cabbage leaves. Snails will be attracted to this during the night and can be disposed of in the morning. If you can't face stamping on them and you like your neighbours too much to throw them over the hedge, just wrap them in newspaper and put them in the dustbin.

To sterilize potting soil

If you use garden soil for potting seedlings, sterilize it first by putting it in a medium oven for an hour. This will kill weed seeds and pests' eggs.

Stinging nettle mulch

Soak a bunch of stinging nettles for three weeks in a bucket of rain water, until thoroughly decomposed. Spread this as a mulch around roots. (If strained, this mixture can be used as an anti-blackfly spray.)

Weed-killer

Clear weeds from a path or patio by pouring boiling salted water over them.

Oven temperatures

	ELECTRICITY		GAS
	F	C	
very cool	225	110	¼
	250	130	½
cool	275	140	1
	300	150	2
moderate	325	170	3
	350	180	4
moderately hot	375	190	5
	400	200	6
hot	425	220	7
	450	230	8
very hot	475	240	9

Food portions

When shopping and cooking, allow the following amounts per person:

soup	½ pint (250 ml)
fish	4–6 oz (125–175 g)
meat without bone	6 oz (175 g)
meat with bone	8 oz (225 g)
green vegetables	4–6 oz (125–175 g)
potatoes	6–8 oz (175–225 g)
rice and pasta as	
accompaniment/starter	2 oz (50 g)
as main course	4 oz (125 g)

Approximate metric equivalents

Use these tables as a guide when converting recipes.

Weight

OUNCES	GRAMMES	OUNCES	GRAMMES
1	25	9	250
2	50	10	275
3	75	11	300
4	125	12	350
5	150	13	375
6	175	14	400
7	200	15	425
8	225	16	450

Liquid

PINTS	LITRES
¼	150 ml
½	275 ml
¾	425 ml
1	575 ml
1½	875 ml
2	1 litre

Game

Rabbits and pigeons are unprotected and available all year. Venison and quail are protected but in season all year. The seasons for other fresh game are as follows:

capercaillie (black grouse)	20 August (1 September in New Forest, Devon and Somerset)–20 December
wild duck	August–February
wild goose	November–December
red (Scottish) grouse	12 August–10 December
hare	1 August–28 February
mallard	1 September–20 December
partridge	1 September–1 February
pheasant	1 October–31 January (10 December in Scotland)
plover	20 August–10 December
ptarmigan (mountain grouse)	20 August–10 December
snipe	12 August–20 December
teal	1 September–20 December
woodcock	1 October–20 December

Fish

Fish are in season – or at their best* – during the following months:

Bass	May to August
Bream	*June to December
Brill	*April to August
Brown trout	*March to September
Carp	October to February

Catfish	September to February
Cod	*October to May
Coley	All year
Conger eel	*March to October
Flounder	February to September
Grey mullet	*July to February
Gurnet	July to April
Haddock	*September to February
Hake	*June to January
Halibut	*August to April
Herring	*June to December
John dory	October to December
Mackerel	October to July
Plaice	*May
Rainbow trout	All year
Salmon	England, Wales, Scotland: February to August; Ireland: January to September
Salmon trout	March to August
Skate	September to April
Smelt	June to September
Sole	All year
Sprat	November to March
Sturgeon	August to March
Turbot	*March to August
Whitebait	*May to July
Whiting	*December to March

Laundering instructions

	Washing Instructions		Fabrics
	Machine	*Hand*	
1 **95°**	VERY HOT to boiling Maximum wash	HAND-HOT or boiling	White cotton and linen without special finishes
	Spin or wring		
2 **60°**	HOT Maximum wash	HAND-HOT	Cotton, linen or rayon without special finishes and with colours fast in hot water
	Spin or wring		
3 **60°**	HOT Medium wash	HAND-HOT	White nylon, white polyester, cotton mixtures
	Cold rinse, short spin or drip-dry		
4 **50°**	HAND-HOT Medium wash	HAND-HOT	Coloured nylon, polyester, cotton and rayon articles with special finishes, acrylic/cotton mixtures, coloured polyester/cotton mixtures
	Cold rinse, short spin or drip-dry		

5 / 40° WARM Maximum wash Spin or wring	WARM	Cotton, linen or rayon articles with colours fast in warm water but not hot water
6 / 40° WARM Minimum wash Cold rinse, short spin; do not wring	WARM	Acrylics, acetates and triacetates, including mixtures with wool, also polyester/wool blends
7 / 40° WARM Minimum wash Spin; do not hand wring	WARM Do not rub	Wool, including blankets, and wool mixtures with cotton or rayon
8 / 30° COOL Minimum wash Cold rinse, short spin, do not wring	COOL	Silk and printed acetates with colours not fast in warm water

Hand wash only

 Do not wash at all

 Bleachable

 Do not bleach

 Cool iron

 Warm iron

 Hot iron

 Do not iron

 Dry cleanable

Do not dry clean

Useful temperatures

	F	C
Freezing	32	0
Useful equivalents	50	10
Set central heating (bedrooms)	60	15
Useful equivalents	68	20
Set central heating (living-rooms)	70	22
Body temperature	98·4	37
Set hot water thermostat	113	55
Boiling	212	100

Useful lengths

These are approximate equivalents.

IMPERIAL	METRIC
½ inch	1 cm
1 inch	2½ cm
4 inches	10 cm
1 foot	30 cm
30 inches	75 cm
1 yard	90 cm
39 inches	1 metre
48 inches	120 cm
54 inches	135 cm
56 inches	140 cm
78 inches	200 cm
90 inches	230 cm
100 inches	260 cm

Bodyweight

STONES	KILOGRAMMES
6	38
7	44·4
8	50·7
9	57·1
10	63·5
11	69·8
12	76·2

Sheet sizes

The standard metric bed is longer than the old imperial bed – 78 inches (200 cm) instead of 75 inches.

The standard metric sheet is 100 inches (260 cm) long.

For a single bed, 30 or 36 inches (75 or 90 cm) wide, you will need sheets 60 or 70 inches (150 or 175 cm) wide.

For a double bed, 54 or 60 inches (135 or 150 cm) wide, you will need sheets 90 inches (230 cm) wide.

Building materials

Timber

THICKNESS		WIDTH	
$\frac{1}{2}$ inch	12 mm	2 inches	50 mm
$\frac{3}{4}$ inch	19 mm	3 inches	75 mm
1 inch	25 mm	4 inches	100 mm
$1\frac{1}{2}$ inches	38 mm	5 inches	125 mm
		6 inches	150 mm
		7 inches	175 mm
		8 inches	200 mm
		9 inches	225 mm

Length. In Britain timber is now cut to standard metric lengths, starting at 0·6 metres, then 0·9, 1·2, 1·5, etc.

NAIL SIZES		DRILL SIZES	
$\frac{5}{8}$ inch	15 mm	$\frac{1}{16}$ inch	1·5 mm
1 inch	25 mm	$\frac{3}{32}$ inch	2·25 mm
$1\frac{1}{4}$ inches	32 mm	$\frac{1}{8}$ inch	3 mm
$1\frac{9}{16}$ inches	40 mm	$\frac{5}{32}$ inch	3·75 mm
2 inches	50 mm	$\frac{3}{16}$ inch	4·5 mm
$2\frac{3}{8}$ inches	60 mm	$\frac{7}{32}$ inch	5·25 mm
$2\frac{1}{3}$ inches	65 mm	$\frac{1}{4}$ inch	6 mm
3 inches	75 mm	$\frac{9}{32}$ inch	6·25 mm

Index

Fontana Paperbacks: Non-fiction

Fontana is a leading paperback publisher of non-fiction, both popular and academic. Below are some recent titles.